THE MURANG'A MURALS

THE MURANG'A MURALS

Edited by Harold F. Miller

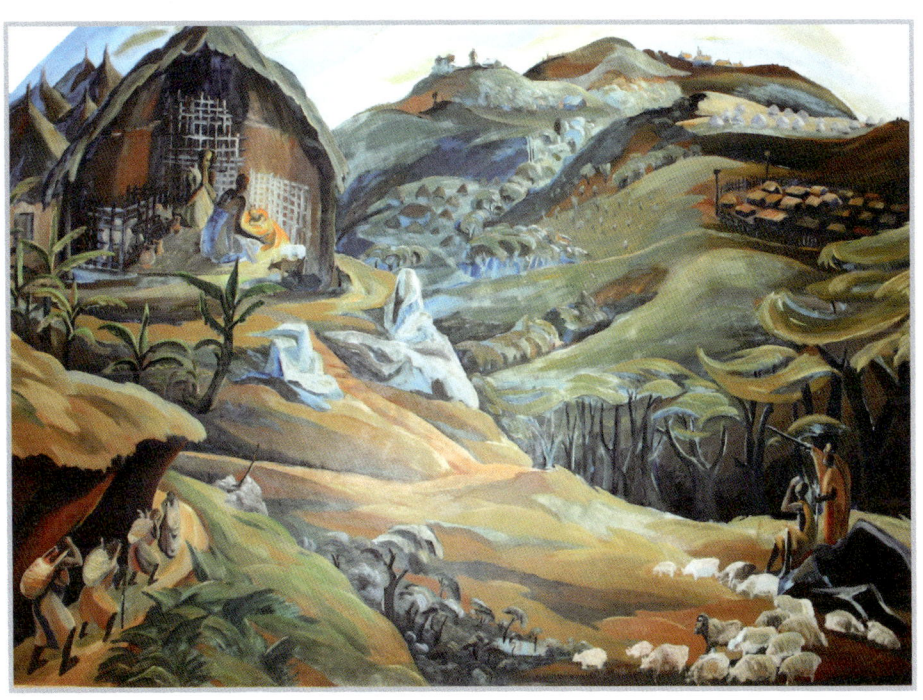

Published by H. F. Miller, Nairobi, Kenya

Produced in association with

MANQA
studio

Nairobi, Kenya
Final editing by Edward Miller
Book design by Edward Miller
Text set in Garamond Premier Pro

This publication is produced as a non-profit initiative.

First Edition
10 9 8 7 6 5 4 3

Printed by CreateSpace
Available from Amazon.com and other retail outlets

CONTENTS

ACKNOWLEDGEMENTS

The contributions of the following persons are acknowledged with appreciation. Gabriel Abraham and Guenet Abraham provided design and editorial advice. Lucas Alube provided access to archival sources. Sister Teresa Marcazzan offered publication advice. Wakuraya Wanjohi, Annetta Miller, and Keith Miller provided design ideas and editorial advice. Rekyaelimoo (Elimo) Njau provided content suggestions and archival materials. Villoo Nowrojee provided editorial assistance and archival materials from her collection on the Murang'a murals and Paa ya Paa Art Centre.

CONTRIBUTORS

James Foster is a retired corporate director and philanthropist with an interest in history, writing, and good governance.

Terry Hirst is an artist and a founder member of Paa ya Paa. He is living in Nairobi, retired.

William Jones is a collector of contemporary diasporic African art who retired in 1999 as Associate Professor of Communication Skills at Rutgers University, Newark, New Jersey. He has also taught in Kenya and Zambia.

Harold F. Miller worked for several decades as a fraternal staff member with ecumenical organizations in the East Africa region, seconded by North American Mennonite agencies. He is living in Nairobi, retired.

Jesse N. K. Mugambi is Professor of Philosophy and Religion at the University of Nairobi and between 2006 and 2009 served as the Director of Starehe Boys Centre.

Phillda Ragland Njau is the coordinator of the International Arts Programme, Paa ya Paa Art Centre, Nairobi.

Pheroze Nowrojee is a Nairobi-born lawyer, poet, and political worker. He was among Paa ya Paa's earliest members and frequents the Murang'a murals as a pilgrim. These poems were written over the 20 years from 1986 to 2006.

Diane Stinton, PhD, is a Canadian who served as the coordinator of the Master of Theology in African Christianity programme at Daystar University, Nairobi.

INTRODUCTION

In 1956, at the height of Kenya's Mau Mau war of independence, a young African Christian artist by the name of Rekyaelimoo (Elimo) Njau was commissioned to paint scenes from the life of Jesus in a church being built as a memorial to Christians who had died in the conflict.

The Murang'a murals appear on the interior north wall of the Saint James and All Martyrs Memorial Cathedral in Murang'a town, known in colonial times as Fort Hall.

There are five murals: *Nativity*, *Baptism*, *The Last Supper*, *Agony in the Garden*, and *Crucifixion*. Each panel is 4.5 metres in width and 3.5 metres in height, with central Kenya's highland landscape providing the setting in which the story of Jesus as recorded in the Christian Gospels is depicted.

Created over a period of several months during the year 1959, the murals retain a striking brightness and clarity more than a half century later.

Tanzanian by birth, Elimo Njau was a student of fine art at Makerere University in Kampala, Uganda, when he was invited to paint the murals. Njau subsequently gained recognition as one of East Africa's foremost artists.

This publication is intended as a modest contribution to reflections on the many aspects of the murals, including the religious, historical, and cultural context in which they were created.

The Saint James and All Martyrs Memorial Cathedral serves as the seat of the Diocese of Mount Kenya Central of the Anglican Church of Kenya.

THE MURALS

I — Nativity

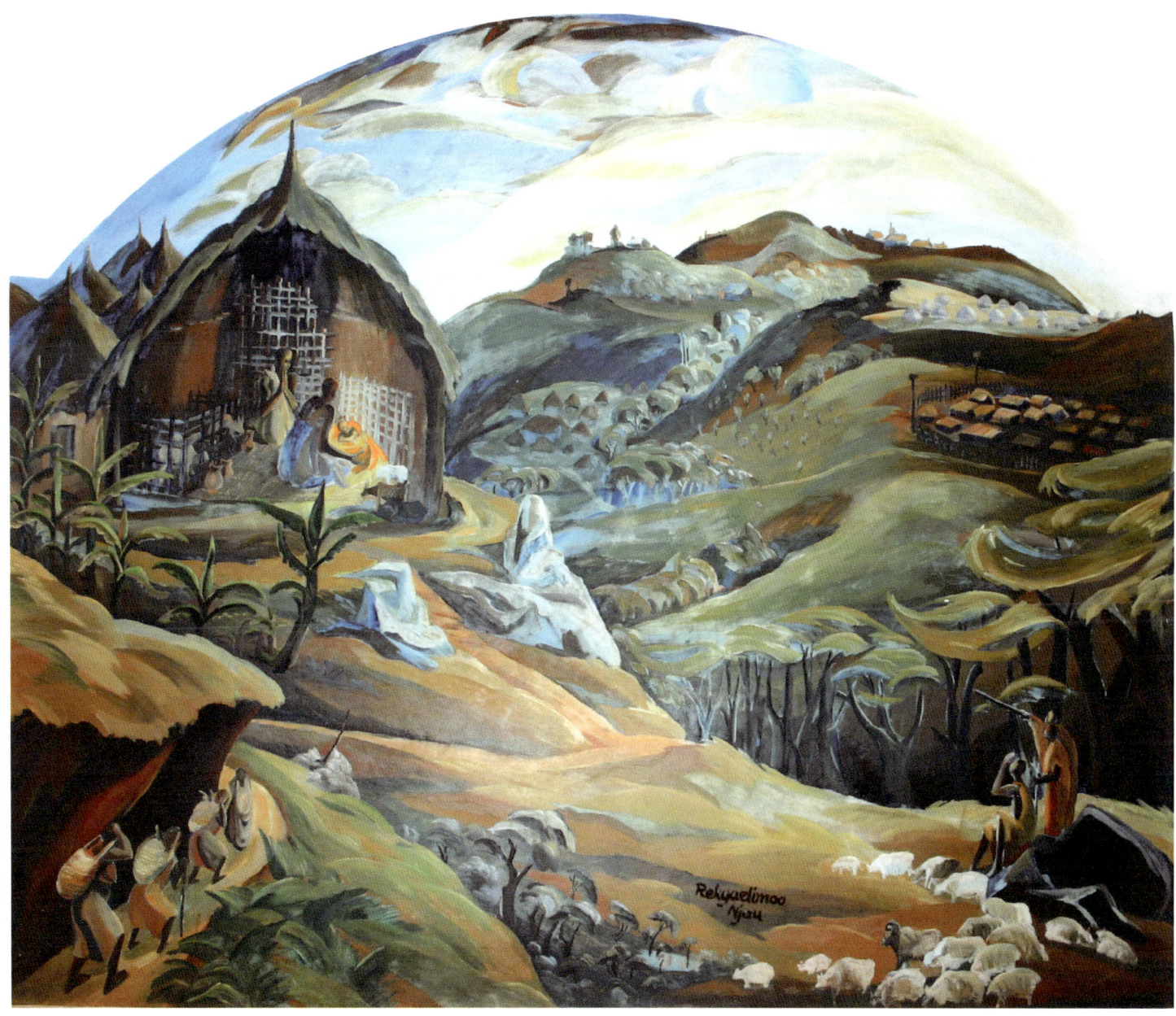

II — Baptism

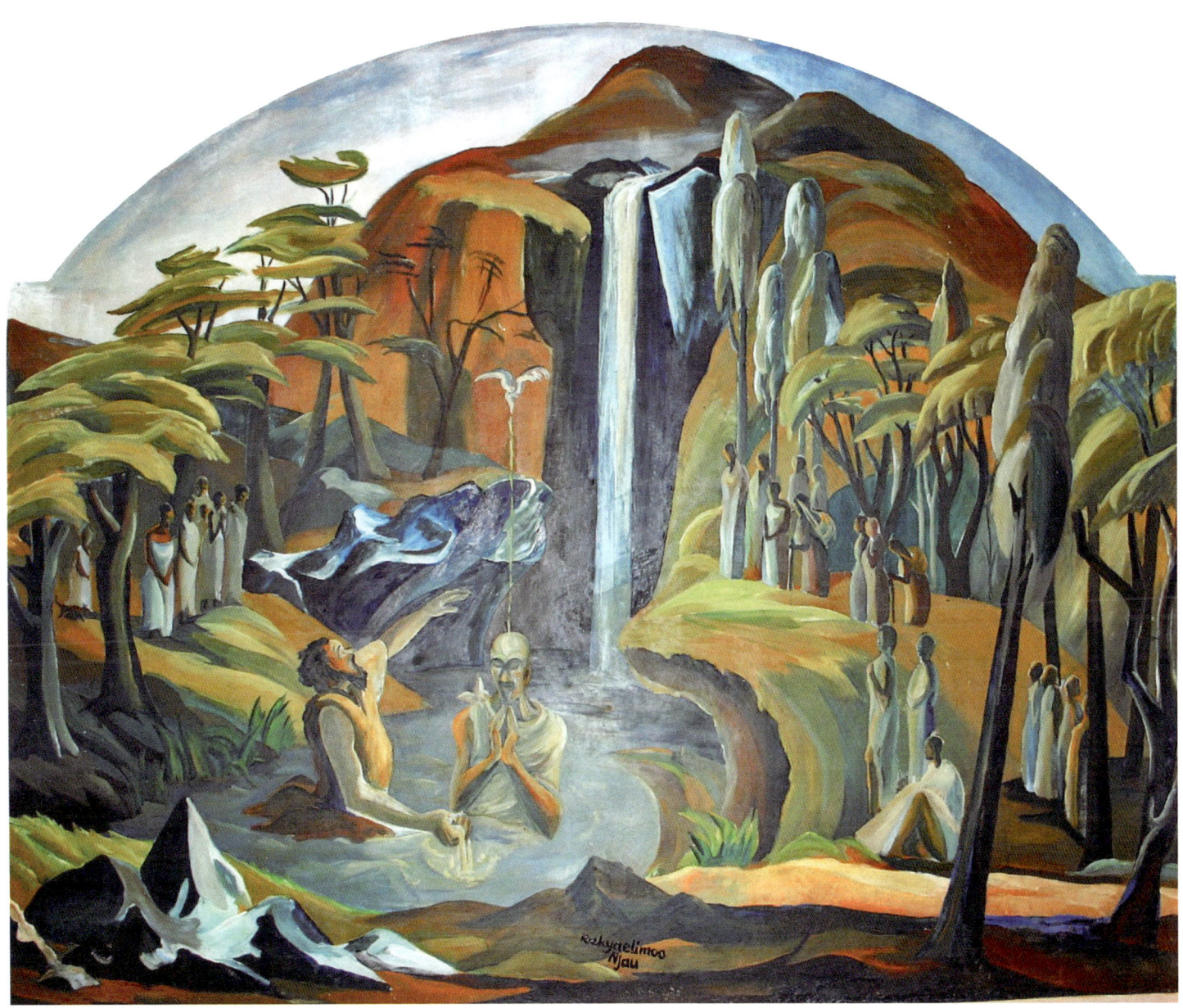

III – The Last Supper

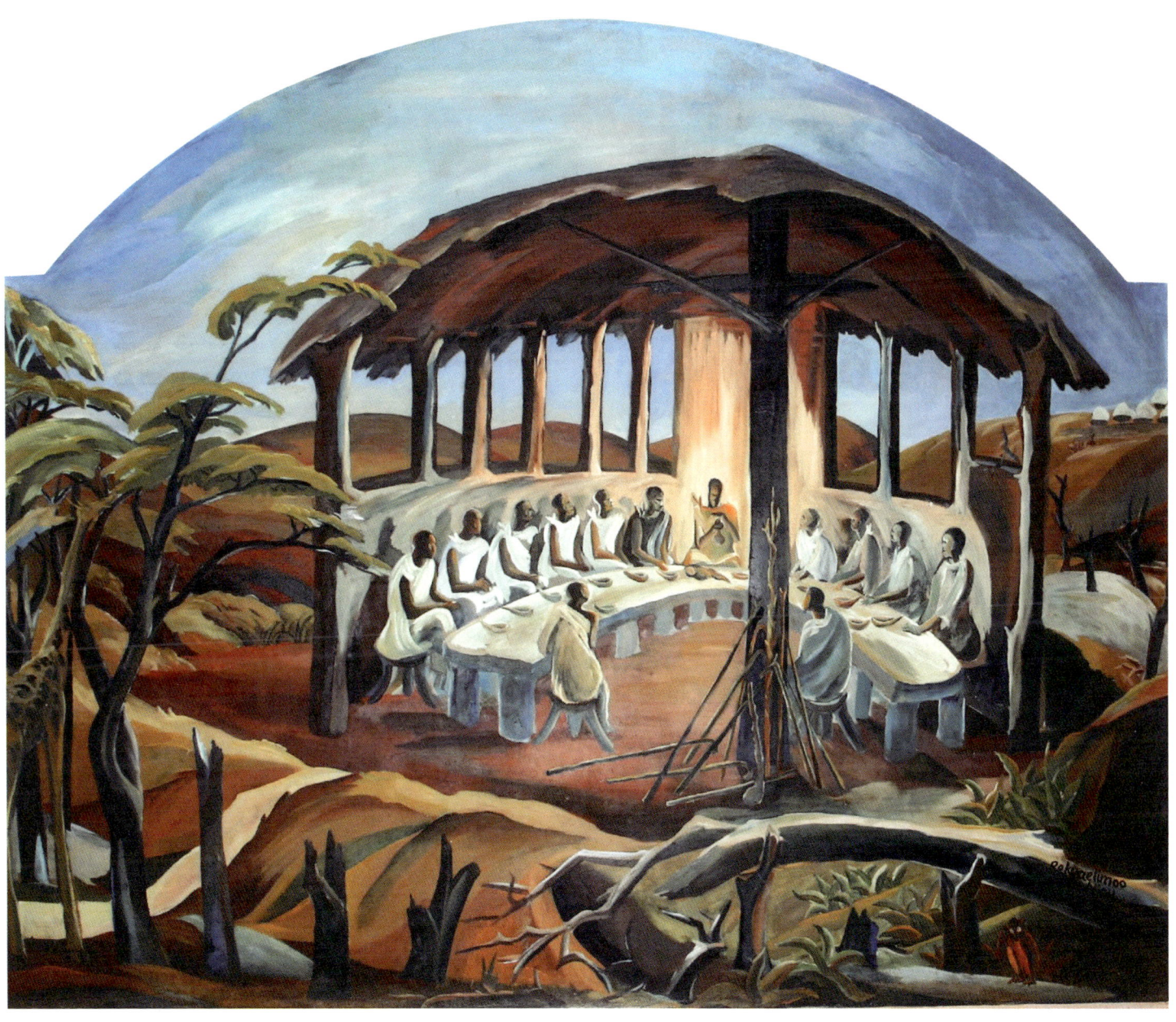

IV — Agony in the Garden

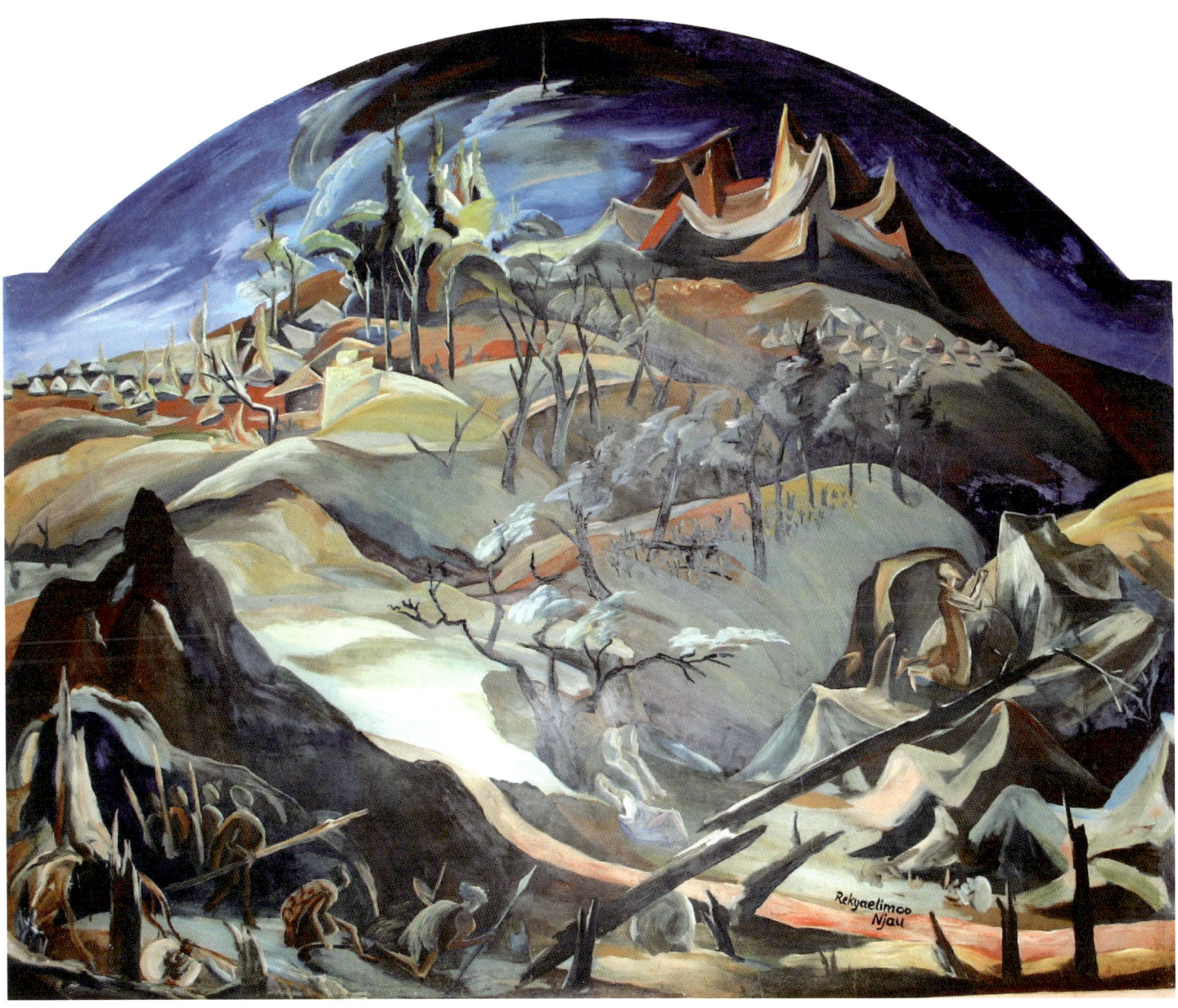

V – Crucifixion

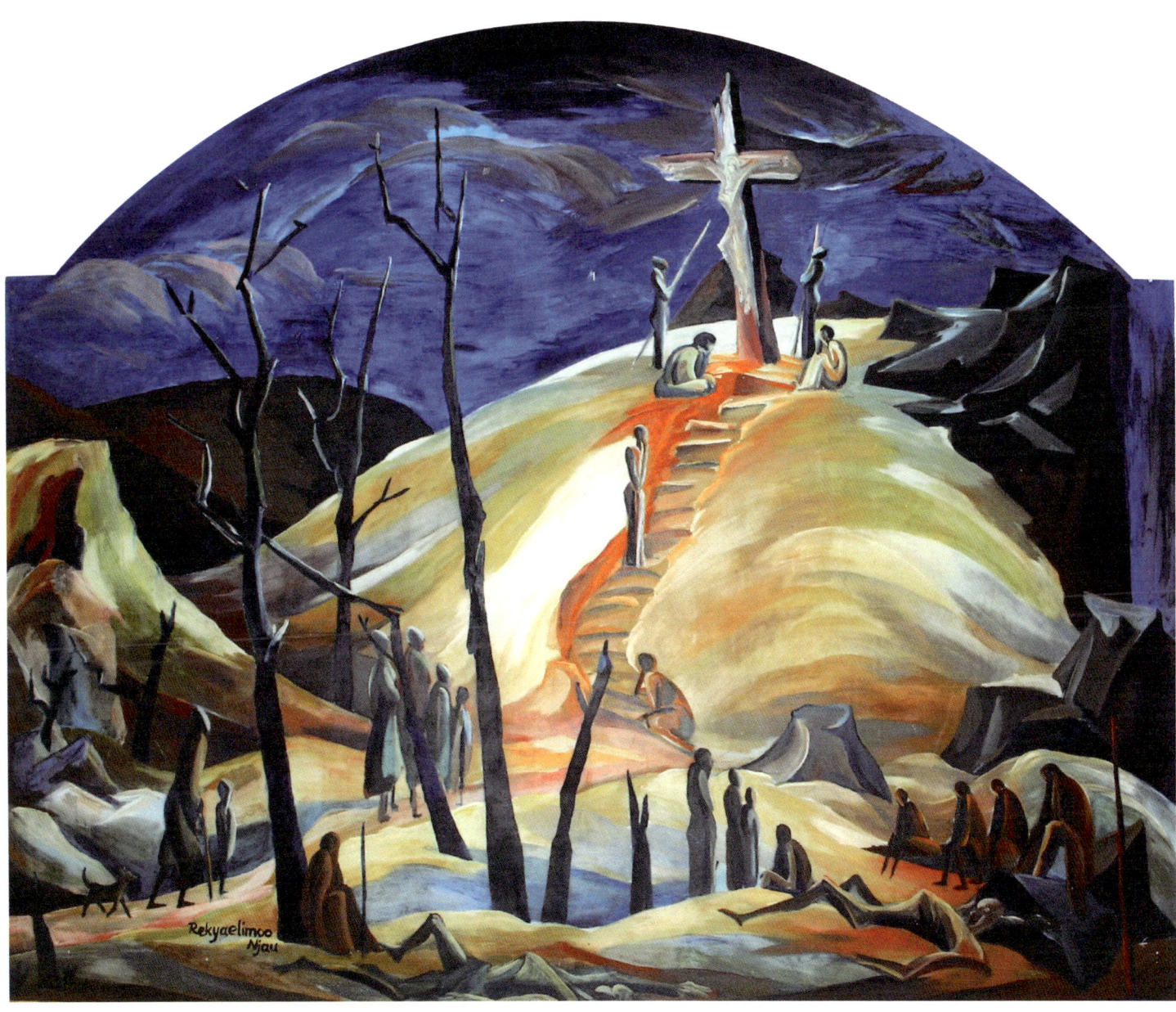

FIVE POEMS

Pheroze Nowrojee

I — Nativity

A hamlet strategically painted in at one edge
Near the pillar
Reminds there is an Emergency on. But
Foreshadowed here is the loss of the imperial will
Now reigning: it is powerless to prevent
This birth of opposing power.

The wire for the searchlights
Will soon be wound back on spools and re-exported,
Recycling the commerce of oppression.
The stockade's timber will shelve shops,
The patrolled land will be vacated,
For all tyrannies are temporary.

In the artist's welling verdance and triumphant palette,
In the generous landscape and the deep assurance of the sky,
In the neglected women of history,
Presently climbing unwatched round a nearby corner,
Is the promise that hope is constantly around,
Before and after this Birth.   ‡

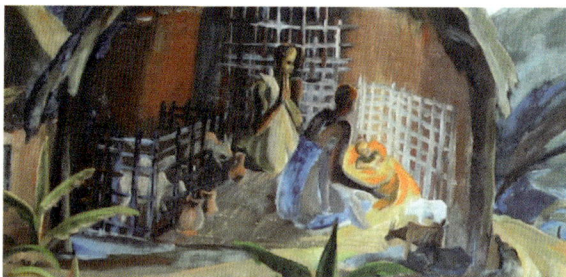

II — Baptism

The land in a serial unfolding
Breaks at the river.

A few curious picnickers,
Some passers by the water's edge,
Stand and idly watch the two strange men.
They are dubious about newcomers
Who speak of the coming of change
In old and distrusted ways;
And even more doubtful
About their avian companion.

But they do not express their views publicly;
In the countryside silence
Has long been the better part of valour.

Yet while obsequies to past gods remain,
In these difficult times anything is worth a try;
Efficacy, not their loyalties as loyalists,
Will decide on the assumption of new superstitions.
But the men in the water
Offer no immediate solutions.

The road, ungravelled, bare of signposts, rolls on,
And the trees lean into the coming years.   ‡

III – The Last Supper

This is an exclusive lodge,
Restricted to members.
There are only twelve, and they are all present,
With their Guest.
The verges of authority, and hierarchy,
Lean against the central pole
(That anticipates the finale).
As befits leaders, even minor ones,
These apostles carry carved sticks
Amidst an unarmed people.
Though it is known that questions
About meeting without a permit
May be raised,
There is no guard.

Someone is about to make – or has made –
An after-dinner speech.
But it does not appear to be one of thanks.
One does not know if, to treason,
Bad manners accrete,
For Judas' departure is abrupt,
And there is no acknowledgement
To those who brought the yams,

Or paid for the brew that had smelled all last week
In the village.
Bar the two, the faces are without ideas,
Their concern for the vintage being handed around,
Or the quality of the conversation, is insufficient.

Only a few can see
That the landscape to our right
Promises little,
And no one notices the owl.   ‡

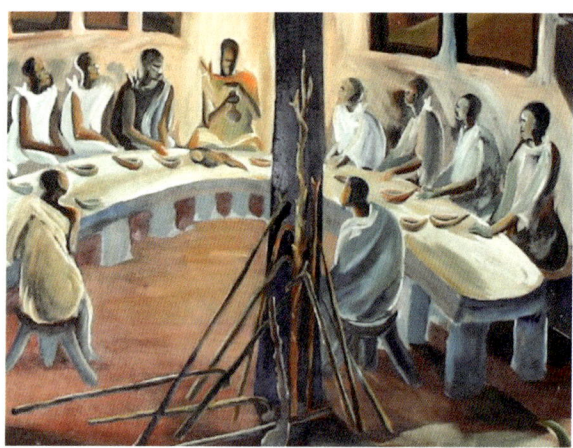

IV – Agony in the Garden

This garden essays a bloom of boulders,
Sheared of loam and flower by the artist's agony.
A special branch disfigures the foreground.
Why are the soldiers hiding?
Why advancing on their knee?
The henchmen of tyranny are hardly humble.
These policemen, and the prosecutors behind them –
For later a trial will be stage-managed –
Are assured of their mandates,
They have their instructions.
Scornful of some distant contingent retribution
From disgruntled victims, or history,
They are fine judges of the bully's art.
So, they are on bended knee
Not to be careful of the single man they can see;
Rather afraid of bungling the assigned apprehension,
Of not remaining useful to those who have sent them.

The person about to be arrested is not alone,
But those who think like Him
Are presently sleeping.
And others,
Not in the picture, and later not before the court,

Are not certain yet that this is the moment
They should speak out; or are debating
Whether Imperial Rome's degrading yoke is still preferable
To the simpler order of an uncompliant prophet.
So the villages at the top of the painting
Remain conveniently in the dark.
Tomorrow some will discuss the arrest
Contextually,
And later, several books, specially from those
Now asleep, like John and Matthew
And one or two others
Will become best-sellers,
Insiders' accounts.

The suspense is not in the outcome of this scene:
Only in the waiting for the acknowledgement
That here wrong is being done.
Somewhere Judas is assessing his profit, his loss,
And someone is choosing Friday's cross.   ‡

V — Crucifixion

The sanctions of the state
Instruct the recalcitrant deviate:
Hammer and nail
Thieves and preachers impale,
Till, like the trees here,
There are twisted frames,
Displaying odd angles for a human body,
Betraying metabolic fatigue.
Our tissue was not made for affixing
To crossed beams or other geometry.
Holes mar the symmetry of perfect feet,
And the preferred palm is unpunctured.

The gravity of this Death is not apparent to all:
A curious dog, tail wagging,
Trots towards the tragedy.
Its concerns are scraps to survive,
As are those of others there.
The attendance is poor,
It is a Friday, a working day,
And the working class cannot attend.
This Friday is not yet a holiday.
Not yet Good.

Not everyone is mourning:
Some say, "He must have done something.
Or the Government would not have charged him."
Listeners nod sagely,
"Just like the other two."

The newspapers will carry it in the Courts Roundup.
But the illustrator is elsewhere,
Covering an opening by Herod;
And in any case, how many can read?
The reporters are not unsympathetic,
But the Subs have their orders,
The report will be noncommittal.
Might not even be carried.
The next-of-kin have been informed;
The body will be released in due course,
Without postmortem or inquest
To inform the future,
Or to still the muted talk of state violence.
Nobody from the Church is present.
It remains silent at the convenient passing
Of an inconvenient voice.

The precipice at Calvary ends these massive arcs of paint,
But a refulgence of red
Drips down the steps
To redeem the future.   ‡

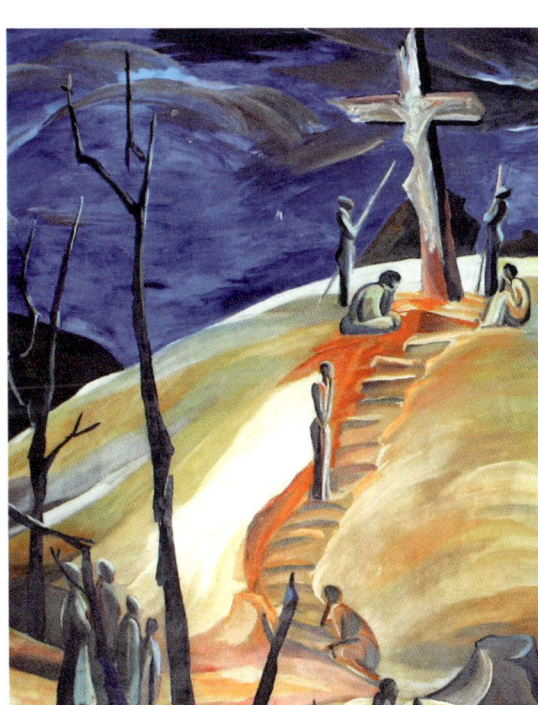

A KENYAN CLEFT STICK: THE HISTORICAL SETTING

Harold F. Miller and James Foster

MURANG'A TOWN is located approximately 80 kilometres to the north-east of Nairobi, the capital city of Kenya. On a hillside just above the town centre stands the Saint James and All Martyrs Memorial Cathedral. It serves as the seat of the Diocese of Mount Kenya Central of the Anglican Church of Kenya.

Inside the cathedral on the wall to the left of the pews, there is a series of five arched murals depicting scenes from the life of Christ. The murals are as striking and imposing as the politico-ecclesiastical context in which they were created.

In 1952, the British Colonial Government of Kenya declared a State of Emergency in some parts of the colony because, in their view, there was a growing atmosphere of lawlessness, as indicated by the murder or mutilation of senior chiefs, who had previously been much respected, and the hamstringing of valuable farm animals of the European farmers.

Following the April 1954 Operation Anvil in the Nairobi area, when all Kikuyu people were rounded up and many were sent to indefinite detention without trial, Anglican Bishop Beecher and District Commissioner John Pinney discussed the possibility of building a church as a permanent memorial to all those Christians who had lost their lives at the hands of the Mau Mau fighters and in other ways since the disturbances started.

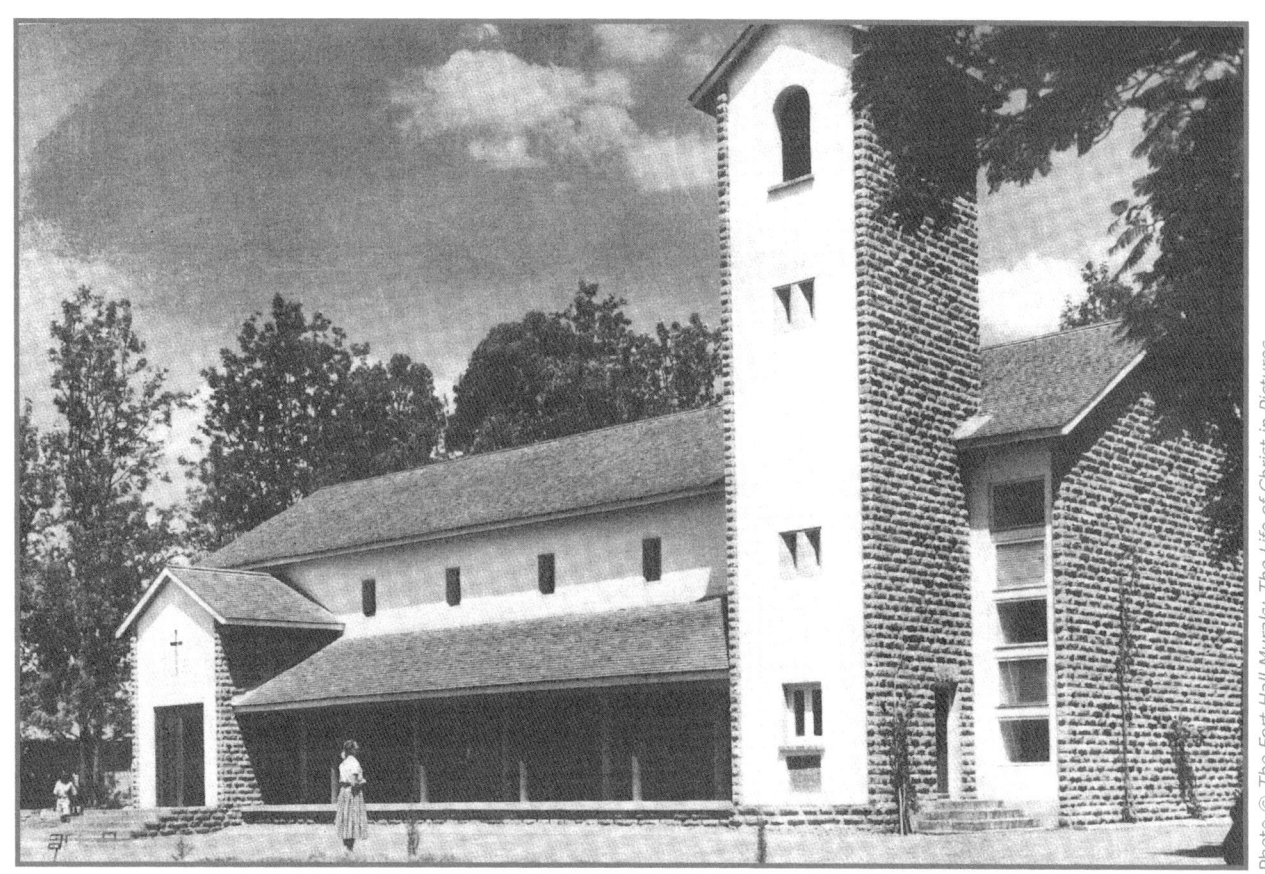

Saint James and All Martyrs Memorial Cathedral, Fort Hall (Murang'a), circa 1960

At that time, a Kenya-born architect, Julian Hill (Associate of the Royal Institute of British Architects), was based in Fort Hall District as a district officer of the Kikuyu Guard. Hill agreed to prepare plans for the building and, once these were approved, Pinney released him from his other duties so that Hill could supervise the construction of the church.

When the Archbishop of Canterbury, the Most Reverend Dr. Geoffrey Fisher, came to East Africa to consecrate the first African bishops at Namirembe Cathedral in Kampala, Uganda, he added five days to his itinerary, enabling him to lay the foundation stone for the memorial church in Fort Hall on 18 May 1955. Etched on the foundation stone that he laid in the presence of a 4,000-strong Kikuyu congregation were the following words:

"In Memory of those who died in the Mau Mau uprising as Martyrs to their faith in Jesus Christ and all those who gave their lives to fight against Mau Mau."

During this time, Archbishop Beecher was making regular visits to Makerere University College in Kampala, Uganda, where Margaret Trowell of the Fine Arts Department had drawn Beecher's attention to a Christian artist by the name of Rekyaelimoo (Elimo) Njau.

Architect Julian Hill invited Njau to visit Fort Hall for the purpose of designing and painting murals in the memorial church, then under construction. Njau was hosted for the duration by the newly appointed Reverend Obadiah Kariuki, serving as rural dean for the Anglican Church in the Fort Hall township.

Fund-raising for the construction and furnishing of the memorial church was coordinated with the Church Missionary Society in London. Substantial funds were raised from Kenyans in the Fort Hall area while European residents in Kenya offered gifts in cash and kind, including furniture for the church.

Small gifts came from people in Britain who had some connection with Kenya, and pews were donated by persons who had lost relatives during the Emergency. Additionally, Beecher arranged for the Church Missionary Society Kenya Mission to guarantee a bank loan enabling the construction of the church to be completed.

Archbishop Beecher consecrated the Saint James and All Martyrs Memorial Church on 12 October 1958. Njau completed his painting of the life-of-Christ murals over one month during the Easter celebrations of 1959. In the same year, the Archbishop of Canterbury consecrated the murals, a celebration recorded on a full back page of the *London Times*, as well as the *Anglican Herald*.

Initiative for the construction of the church in Fort Hall had emanated largely from the European Anglican clergy and European personnel within Kenya's colonial administration. Its construction and its intended purpose as a memorial to martyrs of the Mau Mau rebellion may have indicated, if only implicitly, that the demise of colonial rule in Kenya was already visible on the political horizon.

Kariuki had been recruited to the position of rural dean in the Fort Hall area in part because his European counterparts found it difficult to perform their priestly duties in the face of popular defiance and, latterly, because of the armed resistance of the Mau Mau movement to colonial rule. Subsequently, the appointment of Obadiah Kariuki as the first African bishop to this politically and ecclesiastically sensitive position marked the dawning of an independent African country and launched the unprecedented growth of Anglican Christianity in central Kenya.

According to Kariuki, Murang'a town and its immediate environs, including the slopes of Mount Kenya to the east and the Aberdare Mountain range to the west, served as the arena for armed Mau Mau combatants fighting for the recovery of land that had been excised to benefit European settler farmers.

"When people started actively fighting for their rights in the early fifties, my sympathies were with them," wrote Kariuki. "European church leaders, administrators and settlers were all united in resisting the independence movement. I did not see anything wrong with fighting for one's own freedom in one's own country. What most of us in the church at that time objected to was violence, coercion and, finally, forced oathing to make people join the Mau Mau movement."

According to Kariuki, Africans were "caught in a cleft stick". On the one hand, any African professing the Christian faith could suffer death at the hands of freedom fighters. Almost every morning during the years 1953 and 1954, Kariuki conducted burial services for the "unfortunates" killed either by the colonial administration or by the Mau Mau fighters. On the other hand, Kariuki and many African Christians were clearly antagonistic to colonial rule. Amid these complex nuances and the hesitation of Revivalist Christians to endorse unconventional art, Njau refrained, at the time, from signing the murals.

In 1957, Kariuki sought permission from Colonial Governor Sir Evelyn Baring to visit Jomo Kenyatta, who was then detained in Lokitaung, a semi-desert village located near the Kenya–Sudan border. Kariuki was given permission because Kenyatta had asked for spiritual nourishment. Like Kenyatta, Kariuki was married to a daughter of the ex-Senior Chief Koinange. Kariuki later made representations to Governor Patrick Renison, appointed in October 1959, urging him to release Kenyatta as the only viable means of achieving peace and stability in the country.

Meanwhile, Kenyatta had been moved from Lokitaung to Lodwar and then to Maralal in the Samburu Reserve. Kenyatta was released on 14 August 1961, despite Renison's earlier characterization of him as "a leader to darkness and death". In October 1961, Kenyatta took up the presidency of the Kenya African National Union and so led the process towards complete independence with himself as Prime Minister in 1963 and to republic status with himself as President in 1964.

It was within this volatile transition context that Elimo Njau had been invited to create a Christian artistic statement. He obliged with gusto and passion. The resulting murals can only be described as revolutionary. They represent a dramatic discontinuity with the then prevailing style and principles of religious imagery in Africa, imagery borrowed largely from European precedent and tradition. Against the backdrop of Kenya's political and ecclesial colonial geography, Njau's murals were executed in a resonant Christian African idiom.

‡

THE ARCHBISHOP OF CANTERBURY'S TOUR OF KENYA, 1955

A LONG ROAD JOURNEY through country which a year ago was the haunt of terrorist gangs was undertaken by the Archbishop of Canterbury, Dr. Geoffrey Fisher, for an official function, the laying of the foundation stone of a Memorial Church to the Christian martyrs who died at the hands of Mau Mau. The ceremony took place at the administrative centre of Fort Hall, 60 miles from Nairobi in the heart of the Kikuyu tribal area.

The Primate's message to the Kikuyu people was that only through God could they find true freedom. Dr. Fisher said he had come to encourage the Christian Kikuyu in their faith in Christ, but the knowledge of their "faith unto death" had encouraged him far more than he could encourage them.

The Primate's address was translated sentence by sentence into Kikuyu for the benefit of the 4,000 tribesmen who gathered at the church site. The way from Fort Hall Police Station to the site was lined by 195 Kikuyu Tribal Policemen and similar groups of Tribal Police guarded the ten-mile road to Kahuhia where the Archbishop later had luncheon at an Anglican mission and teacher centre. Among the crowd were contingents of Christians from seven pastorates of Fort Hall and Embu districts, and the African Christian Churches and Schools.

On arrival at Fort Hall Dr. Fisher inspected a Guard of Honour of the Kenya Police. Then, attended by the Bishop of Mombasa, the Right Rev. L. J. Beecher; two African Assistant Bishops, the Rt. Rev. Obadiah Kariuki and the Rt. Rev. Festo Olang'; his chaplain the Rev. Gilbert Baker; the Rev. Alan Page, Rural Dean of Fort Hall; and the Rev. Eshban Gitura, the Archbishop moved in procession from the police station to a raised dais in front of the foundation stone from which the service was conducted by the Bishop of Mombasa. After a short service the archbishop laid the stone which will support the church tower and then addressed the congregation.

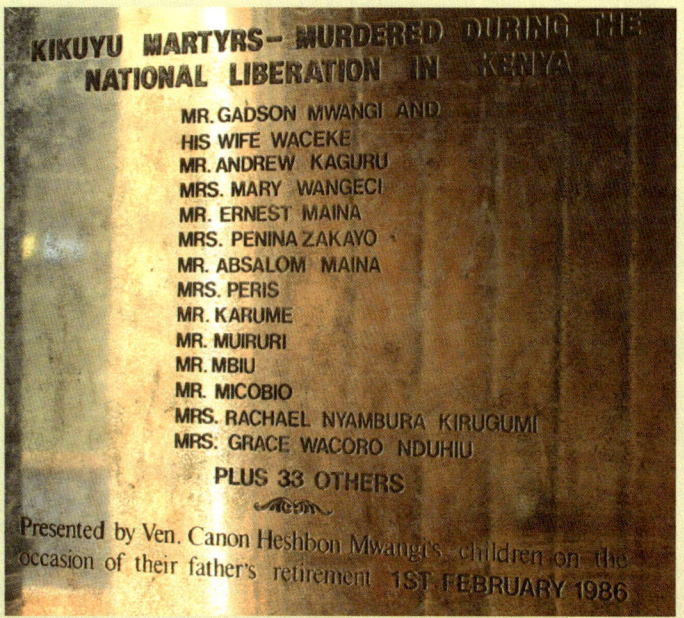

Plaque in the cathedral listing the Kikuyu martyrs "plus 33 others"

"I have been in many parts of the world," the Primate said, "but in all my travels nothing has so moved me as this gathering here. Here we are at the very heart of the struggle of Jesus Christ to deliver men from evil. In the hearts of every one of you this struggle is being fought out."

"How I long to be able to meet, face to face, those who have been led into the hateful ways of the Mau Mau," Dr. Fisher continued. "Those who are of this evil belief are only destroying good things. They are destroying the best of your people here; they are destroying the true advance to freedom of the Kikuyu people; they are destroying life while Jesus Christ comes to give us life more abundant.

"Only the faith of Christ would stand firm against evil and overcome it. Those men in whose memory the church would stand had died for their faith and had died full of hope because they had passed into the Kingdom of God and had found their Saviour.

"The news of these martyrdoms and your faith as you stood firm has gone all round the world. Far away in England we have given thanks to God for them, and have been strengthened in our faith," Dr. Fisher continued.

"I have been all my life a man of peace and have lived in quietness. I have never had to face the kind of decision that you have faced, of life and death, and it is therefore very very humbly that I speak to you, only praying that if such a decision came to me I might be as faithful as you have been," he continued.

"So I have come as far as I can to encourage you, my friends, in this faith in Christ, but, in very truth, you encourage me far more than I can ever encourage you by this knowledge of your faith unto death."

Dr. Fisher then moved around the edge of the crowd, meeting the Christian congregations of the various areas and chiefs and leaders of the Kikuyu people. As he raised his hand in greeting, the 4,000 tribesmen broke spontaneously into a Kikuyu hymn of rejoicing, which continued long after the Primate had left.

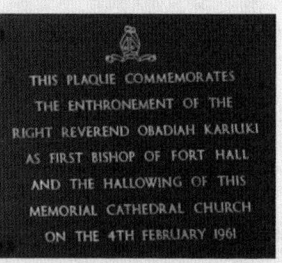

THIS PLAQUE COMMEMORATES THE ENTHRONEMENT OF THE RIGHT REVEREND OBADIAH KARIUKI AS FIRST BISHOP OF FORT HALL AND THE HALLOWING OF THIS MEMORIAL CATHEDRAL CHURCH ON THE 4TH FEBRUARY 1961

Plaque in the cathedral commemorating the elevation of Reverend Obadiah Kariuki to the position of bishop

An appeal for funds is to be launched to enable the Memorial Church to be completed. Designed by a young Kenya-born architect, Mr. Julian Hill, A.R.I.B.A., who is now serving in Fort Hall as a Kikuyu Guard Officer, the church will seat about 240 people. Its most striking feature will be an open aisle on one side, which will be sheltered only by a verandah roof. The aisle on the other side will be decorated with large murals of religious subjects designed by students at Makerere University College in Uganda.

Department of Information,
Kenya Colony, May 1955

IMAGES OF THE INVISIBLE GOD IN MURANG'A

Diane Stinton

NESTLED IN the rolling hills of Murang'a, the cathedral of the Anglican Church of Kenya stands as a living tribute to the martyrs of the violent Mau Mau rebellion against British rule in Kenya. Appropriately named, the Saint James and All Martyrs Memorial Cathedral commemorates all those who died as a result of the 'Emergency' from 1952 to 1960 – European settlers, British soldiers and police, African civilians, and Mau Mau freedom fighters.

Contemporary accounts generally depict Mau Mau as savage 'natives' murdering 'civilized' British settlers, with the British government stepping in to playing a benevolent role of protecting the empire's kith and kin. Contrary to this perception, historians explain the Mau Mau movement more accurately as an internecine war, largely confined to the Kikuyu people, between the rebels and the 'loyalists', those who sided with the British against the Mau Mau.

Some loyalists were deliberately enticed and trained by the British as armed vigilantes, or Home Guards; others did not share the values of the Mau Mau fighters and opposed violence as the means to seek independence. In the end, 32 European settlers and fewer than 200 British soldiers and police died in the rebellion. By contrast, over 1,800 African civilians were murdered by Mau Mau and many hundreds more disappeared, without their bodies being found. Official figures record the total number of Mau Mau rebels killed at 12,000, but the actual figure is likely over 20,000.

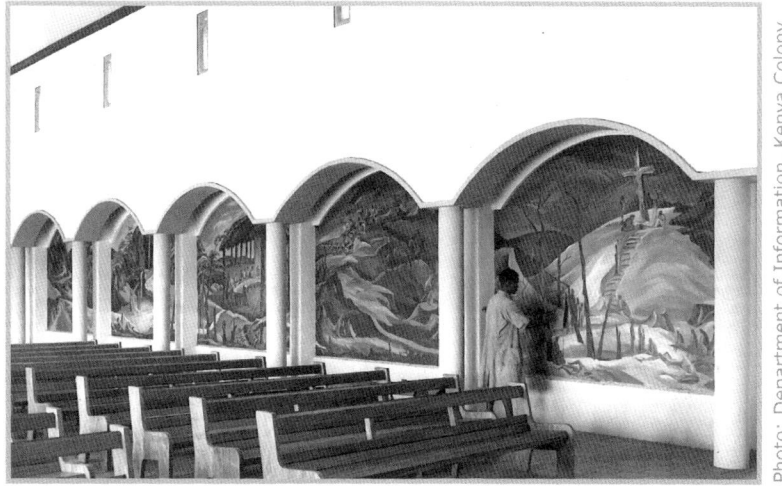

Elimo Njau working on the Crucifixion mural in 1959

Aside from this sheer loss of life, the intensity of the struggle tore apart the very fabric of Kikuyu society. Throughout the course of the rebellion, the British held over 150,000 Kikuyu – whether convicted or simply suspected supporters of Mau Mau – behind wire in detention camps. As David Anderson summarizes, "In the midst of the war, draconian anti-terrorist laws were introduced suspending the human rights of suspects, imposing collective punishments, facilitating detention without trial, permitting the seizure of property of convicts, and vastly extending the death penalty to a wide range of offences. Between 1952 and 1956, when the fighting was at its worst, the Kikuyu districts of Kenya became a police state in the very fullest sense of that term." Without a doubt, the Mau Mau rebellion was one of the darkest moments in Kenyan history.

At the height of this war, in 1956, a young African Christian artist was called and commissioned to paint scenes from the life of Christ in what was then a memorial chapel built in Fort Hall, later renamed Murang'a. The artist slipped into the turmoil in this district, where some of the worst fighting in the civil war took place.

As a guest of Bishop Obadiah Kariuki, he spent several months learning the local landscape, absorbing the contours of nature, culture, and politics. In the process, he interacted with British settlers and soldiers (who took him as the church sweeper), with Mau Mau oath-takers and loyalist oath-haters, and with East African Revival 'brethren' who 'X-rayed' him on his experience of salvation. In 1959, he returned to undertake the actual painting of the chapel wall. Within a single month, and with the bishop praying for him daily, he completed his mission, leaving – unsigned – five stunning, 3.5 metre-by-4.5 metre murals depicting key moments in the life of Christ.

Fifty years later, the murals remain virtually identical in quality and the young artist has grown in prominence to become one of East Africa's foremost artists: Rekyaelimoo (Elimo) Njau. Tanzanian by birth, Njau was studying fine art at Makerere University in Kampala, Uganda, when architect Julian Hill, who was also district commissioner at the time, invited him to paint the murals. With an injunction from the church elders (East African Revivalists) not to paint large figures so that people might worship them instead of God, Njau sought to let the landscape tell the story of Christ's coming – not only as recorded in the Gospels, but also, quite clearly, Christ's coming to Murang'a, the very heartland of Mau Mau.

The first mural depicts the nativity scene, set within verdant, undulating hills dotted with traditional Kikuyu villages and settler homes on the horizon. Strikingly, a distant hillside is dominated by the dark fence posts, watchtowers, and barracks of a British detention camp. Closer by, local shepherds point out the nativity, while a line of women, struggling under the heavy loads of their *viondo* (Kikuyu baskets), ascend the hill, evidently oblivious to the miraculous birth in their midst. Perhaps most radically, especially for the year 1959, Jesus is portrayed as an African babe, wrapped in

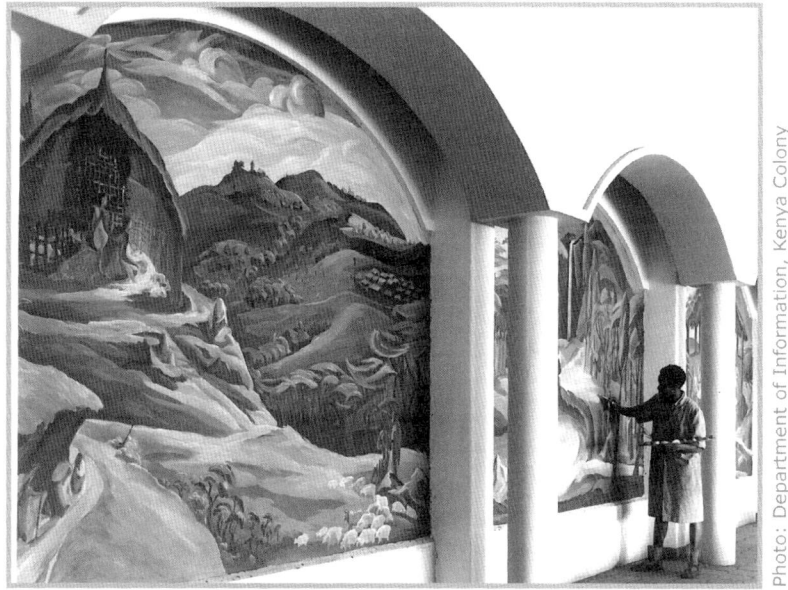

Elimo Njau painting the murals in 1959

swaddling cloths of vibrant orange, worshipped by ebony-skinned parents, and gazed upon by goats and sheep within a typical thatched Kikuyu home.

The second scene is that of Jesus's baptism, set within a pool below Chania Falls, a traditional site for Kikuyu initiation into adulthood. While the figure of John the Baptist has a full head of hair and beard, the figure of Jesus appears subtly head-shaven and waist deep in the river, as customary for initiation candidates. The power of the Spirit, hovering dove-like above Jesus, blends in with the power of the waterfall, and its 'thunder' is suggestive of the voice of God in the biblical scene. The arc of the Baptist's arm mirrors the curve of the landscape, together placing the focus on Jesus as the centre of the picture. Once again, it appears an ordinary scene, with some bystanders attentive to the event while others are apparently unaware.

The Last Supper, the subject of the third mural, is portrayed in a *thingira*, a Kikuyu hut in which matters of consequence are considered. Jesus and his disciples, one of whom conspicuously wears a dark robe, feed from local calabashes and drink wine from a *ruhia*, the ceremonial horn. The centre pole of the hut resembles a cross, anticipating Calvary. Against this pole lean the walking sticks of the disciples, one of which stands out as a *rungu*, the local wooden club used as a weapon, suggesting the violence to come by Judas's hand. Significantly, an owl lurks in the lower right corner, prophetic symbol of the ominous circumstances in both the biblical and the local context. Additionally, in this middle mural, the lush foliage, on which a giraffe quietly feeds, begins to give way to darkened tree stumps and arid hills.

In the fourth scene, Gethsemane is depicted unmistakably against the local context of Murang'a. The dark, distinctive crags of Mount Kenya dominate the background, while Kikuyu villages blaze with fire below. Lower down, Jesus prays alone on a ridge – a solitary, vulnerable figure, seemingly about to be swallowed up by tomb-like rocks, and surrounded by a foreboding landscape of lifeless vegetation. The presence of death pervades the foreground, with skulls littering the dead forest floor and spear-and-skin-clad Mau Mau emerging furtively from a cave in the rocks.

Death then nearly fills the final mural of the Crucifixion: the stark, broken silhouettes of tree-trunks; the sinister, lifeless hills of rock surrounding the scene; the gnarled limbs of the two thieves, sprawled on the ground exposed to die, in keeping with Kikuyu custom, rather than on crosses beside Jesus; and finally, the lone figure of Christ on the cross. Yet while death clearly dominates the scene, hope is nonetheless present, as indicated by the surrounding dark shades being suffused with an intense yellow light that is not from the sky. A few individuals mourn at the foot of the cross, while others – a woman on her knees, an old man with a child and a dog – make their way up the hillside to the cross. There, Jesus appears in the highest position, almost ephemeral, sharing in but triumphant over the suffering below, a fitting tribute to those Kikuyu martyred for their faith.

In this striking portrayal of Jesus entering Murang'a during the plight of Mau Mau, Elimo Njau clearly demonstrates how "the Christ becomes 'one-of-us', embracing the religio-cultural, political, and ecological realities of the day". In the artist's own words, "I learned to see Christ as one among us."

‡

THE ARTIST IN THE RELIGIOUS CONTEXT

Jesse N. K. Mugambi

THIS PUBLICATION CELEBRATES the role of art as an expression of African Christian theology during the colonial and post-colonial periods in Kenya. In 1959, Rekyaelimoo (Elimo) Njau painted five murals on the inside walls of the Saint James and All Martyrs Memorial Cathedral located in Murang'a, Kenya. These murals are the most explicit and earliest expression of contextual Christian theology by an African artist from the East Africa region, in this generation. In the paintings, the artist links the suffering of the people of central Kenya living under the British colonial administration during the State of Emergency (1952–1959) to the suffering, crucifixion, and death of Jesus Christ in Palestine under imperial Roman rule, conspired by the stultifying and self-righteous Jewish religious leaders.

Elimo Njau had obviously studied and to a significant extent internalized the doctrinal essence of the Christian message. As a gifted artist, he then gave visual expression of his understanding, deploying a distinctly African idiom at once relevant to the Christian faith and resonant with the historical context of African Christians in central Kenya. He adhered to the most stringent demands of his chosen medium, and decades later those murals remain resplendent, in full colour, as when they were initially painted.

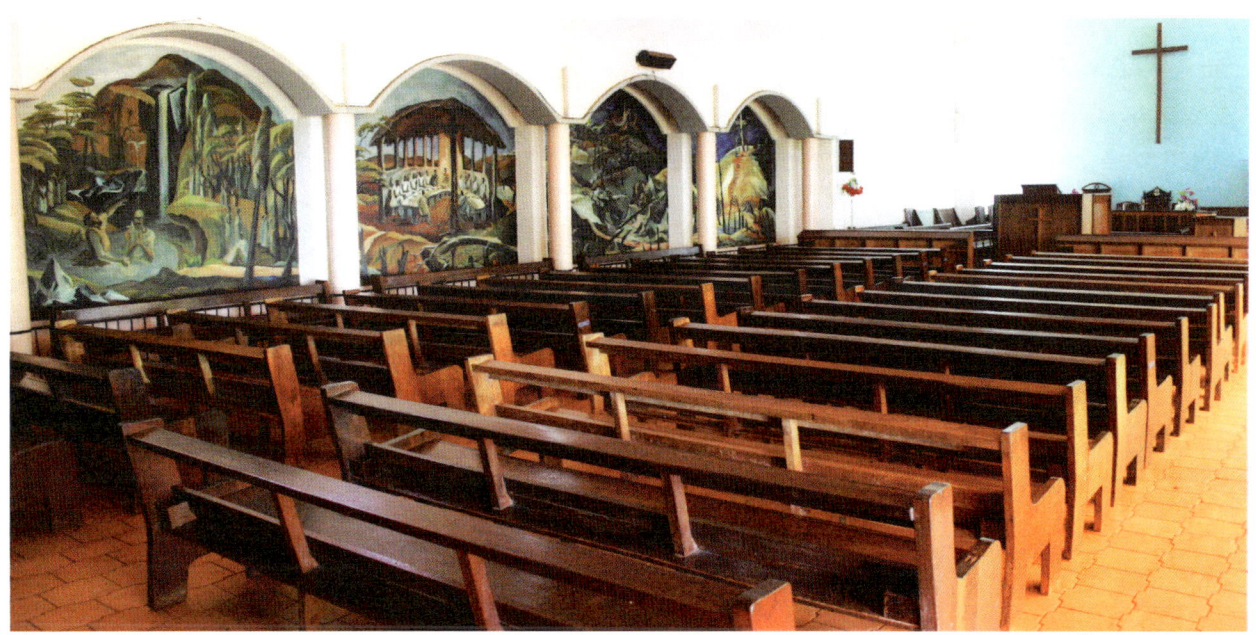

Main sanctuary of Saint James and All Martyrs Memorial Cathedral

During the 1970s, Njau's artwork enjoyed exposure in serial exhibitions staged at the Paa ya Paa Art Gallery in Nairobi. Among many other engagements, he was commissioned to paint the canvas banner for the Third Assembly of the All Africa Conference of Churches, held in Lusaka, Zambia in May 1974. The following year, he painted a banner for the Fifth Assembly of the World Council of Churches, convened in Nairobi in November.

At that time, the theme 'liberation' pervaded much of the substantive social and political discourse throughout the continent. Ironically, there was scepticism, even contempt, in some quarters towards any positive allusion to or use of the adjective 'African'. In that regard, the encounter and interaction with Njau's art was immensely refreshing and encouraging. Regretfully, many decades after Njau's contextual breakthrough, Christian theological reflection in African idioms and thought forms has yet to become normative in discourses on African Christian theology and liturgy.

John V. Taylor, a long-serving British missionary in East Africa and later General Secretary of the Church Missionary Society, had already recognized this lacuna in the 1950s. According to him, missionary-led Christianity had tended towards the creation of denominational replicas, with credentials that could be taught, examined, and regurgitated in classroom settings. Taylor was among the first missionaries to raise the question "What does African Christianity contribute to the world church?"

Concomitantly, colonial governance systems in Kenya – as elsewhere in Africa, imposed from afar – were serving the goals of the metropolis, not the needs of colonial subjects. How do apparently competing or opposing religious understandings, political systems, and cultural expressions come to terms with each other in the midst of highly conflicted and contradictory contexts?

Taylor and some African theologians after him were reaching for an alternative but somewhat elusive quality of consciousness, for which Taylor used the term "presence". Njau exercised his artistic genius, his African thought patterns, and his excellent academic training to create a timeless commentary on a historical turning point in Kenya, juxtaposing liberation with oppression; imported Christian praxis with indigenous religious and cultural norms; African religio-cultural identity with biblical narratives; missionary teachings with African responses; African religious dynamism with western missionary initiatives; and a peasant world view with imperial ideology. These disparate, unlikely cultural and religious elements he fused into a holist proximity, rendering them 'present' to each other.

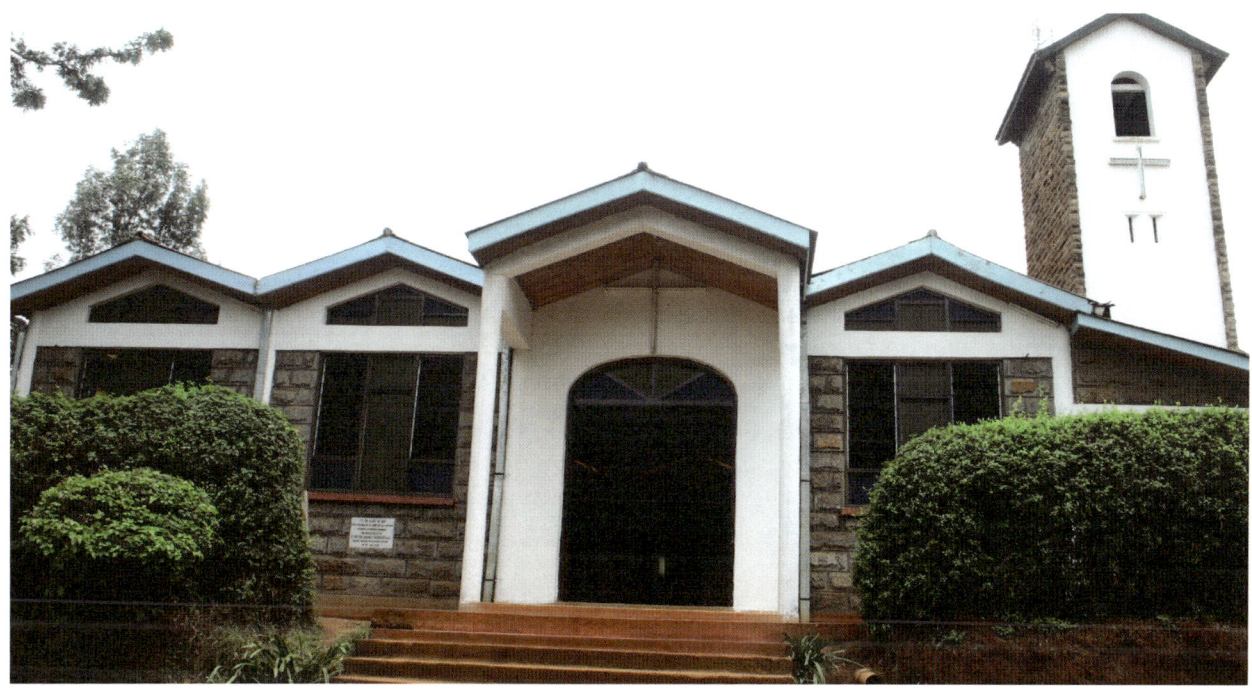

Saint James and All Martyrs Memorial Cathedral

Elimo Njau's murals are self-explanatory. They are imbued at once with the sombre mood brooding over the Holy Week in Jerusalem and with the pervasive political and social tensions during the State of Emergency in Kenya. Until the debut of Njau's murals in Murang'a, African art and music had been considered either irrelevant to or inconsistent with the norms inculcated by missionary teaching. With these paintings, he demonstrated that African art can and does serve as an effective expression of African Christianity and does as well comment in articulate fashion on Africa's political and religio-cultural reality.

While Taylor was writing and teaching at Bishop Tucker Theological College in Mukono, Uganda, Elimo Njau was studying fine art at Makerere University College in Kampala. Many of Njau's lecturers and their peers across Africa were Taylor's compatriot contemporaries, anxious to impart to their African students the 'best' education from their own expatriate perspectives. These included N. Q. King, F. B. Welbourn, Roland Oliver, Geoffrey Parrinder, Thomas Beetham, S. G. Williamson, and Carey Francis, among others. Roland Oliver's book *The Missionary Factor in East Africa* provides the perceptual setting for Njau's murals.

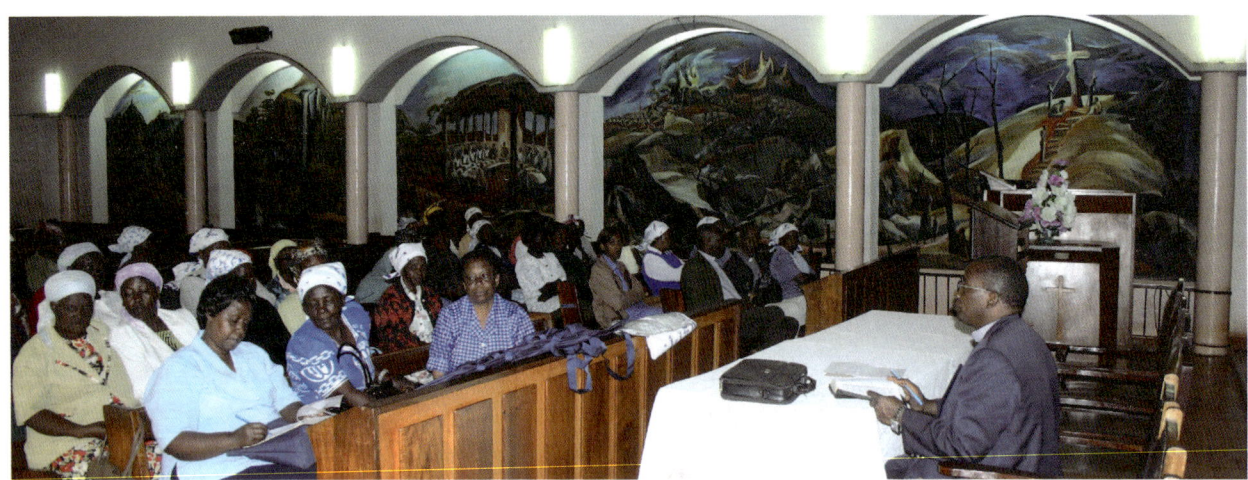

Saint James and All Martyrs Memorial Cathedral

Njau was a student at a time when the 'wind of change' throughout Africa was blowing relentlessly towards political independence. There were few windbreaks to check its thrust. Some expatriates recognized that the time for change had come, but were loathe to declare their ideological positions openly. Others lobbied in London, favouring the cause of African subjects against the British settlers and administrators. But a widely held perspective of Europeans in East Africa, irrespective of religious affiliation, was that struggles for national liberation were evil and subversive, undermining the viability of the colonial state.

Despite this generally negative atmosphere, Njau bravely expressed his thoughts through an incisive artistic medium. Perhaps his Tanganyikan and Lutheran background buoyed him along as the 'outsider' in a highly sensitive social and political environment. Perhaps his status as a 'commissioned artist' provided him the kind of freedom that would have been more problematic for a non-commissioned Kenyan artist.

Did either missionary clerics or colonial officials perceive Njau's paintings as subtly subversive? Were African Christians aware and appreciative of the message expressed in the murals? Available evidence suggests that perceptions were various, mixed, and hesitant. Under the circumstances, the murals remained unsigned until 2006.

Njau's murals were created in a setting exuding nationalist resistance against colonial rule during the 1950s. As a Crown Colony, Kenya was administered from the Colonial Office in London through the Governor, who was resident in Nairobi, the colonial capital. British settlers in Kenya were determined to keep the most fertile areas under their control, land which they called the 'White Highlands'. Africans were evicted from their ancestral homes, confined to less fertile areas, which the settlers called 'Native Reserves', and used as sources of cheap labour for the settlers' farms and ranches. Settlers were regarded as British 'citizens', while Kenyan natives were considered to be British 'subjects'. The imperial citizens could enjoy democracy, but the colonial subjects could not. Schooling was available up to university level for the citizens, but a subject was fortunate to gain access to four years of schooling.

During the 1940s, settlers were determined to keep Kenya British. At the same time, Kenyan nationalists were determined to ensure that the principles of freedom and democracy, so dear to the imperial rulers and citizens, would also be enjoyed, at any cost, by the colonial subjects. In Njau's murals, the 'African disciples' of the 'African Jesus' are nationalists, loyal to their Master. Their enemies are traitors who betray them to the imperial rulers and their local potentates. Despair hovers over the entire land, culminating in the crucifixion, a scene charged with high-voltage hermeneutic power. Anyone who has suffered direct imperial subjugation, anywhere in the world, will immediately identify with the characters in Njau's murals, even in the absence of commentary.

Njau was among the first generation of African students at Makerere University College. Elsewhere on the continent there were two similar colleges: Fourah Bay College in Sierra Leone and Fort Hare College in South Africa. It was in these institutions that the most brilliant young Africans were admitted for training within the British Commonwealth. Many first-generation African leaders were trained in these institutions, with some joining politics while most opted for other professions. Njau became a professional artist and has remained so throughout his life. Among his renowned contemporaries at Makerere were luminaries such as Professor Ali Mazrui, Professor John Mbiti, Professor Joseph Maina Mungai, Professor Okot p'Bitek, Professor Ngugi wa Thiongo, Professor David Rubadiri, and Professor John Ruganda. The list is long. Elimo Njau is the most renowned among the artists, although others such as Francis Naggenda also made significant contributions in painting and sculpture.

Religion is integral to culture. Ritual is always an appropriation of materials, processes, and spaces for the symbolic expression of joy, sorrow, fear, and hope within a community. In the absence of art, religion becomes personalized and internalized. Njau makes this point brilliantly. The murals in the Saint James and All Martyrs Memorial Cathedral have served as an artistic crucible in which the Christian message became present to and conversant with the political and cultural challenges of the day.

Now, not long after the fiftieth anniversary of the murals, Elimo Njau is acknowledged with appreciation and respect as a champion of African religious art in a class of his own.

‡

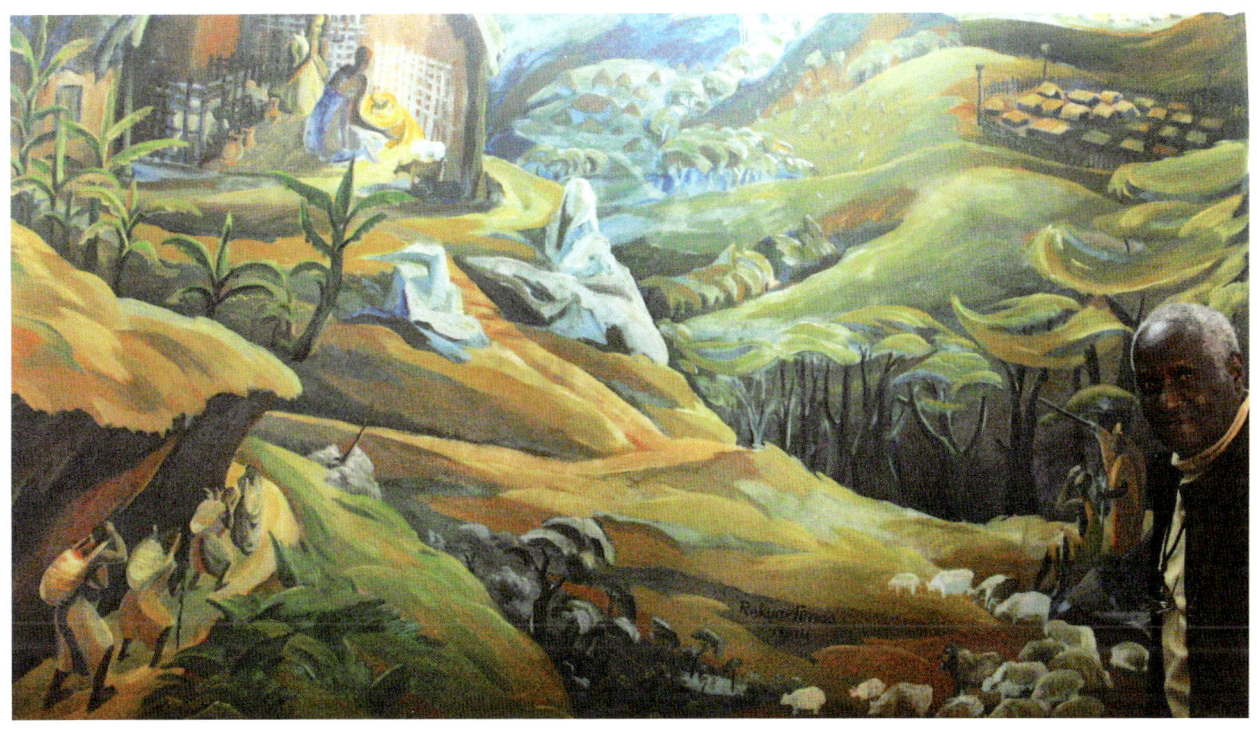

Elimo Njau with the first mural panel

PERSONALITY, RELIGION, AND POLITICS IN THE ART OF ELIMO NJAU

William Jones

FROM NAIROBI, Murang'a is on the north-bearing Murang'a Road towards Mount Kenya into Central Province. It is not a place on tourists' itineraries. Until 1965 and before independence in 1963, Murang'a was called Fort Hall. It was and remains a provincial government administration centre. Its significance to me was that it was the place where Elimo Njau had painted his famous Fort Hall murals, works I would not actually see until August 2002. I had been content, it seemed, to have the knowledge of their existence simply as information, part of the folklore I had gradually accumulated about Njau since first encountering him at Makerere University College in Kampala, Uganda, in 1961.

In my eight weeks at Makerere, preparing to undertake a two-year teaching contract in an East African secondary school, the art department became a draw. With some regularity, I walked into a studio classroom, just to see what was going on. The philosophy that directed instruction announced itself almost immediately. It was clear to me even on the first brief visit: "Your environment is rich," the department seemed to say. "Use it. Subjects and inspiration are available in the most improbable places."

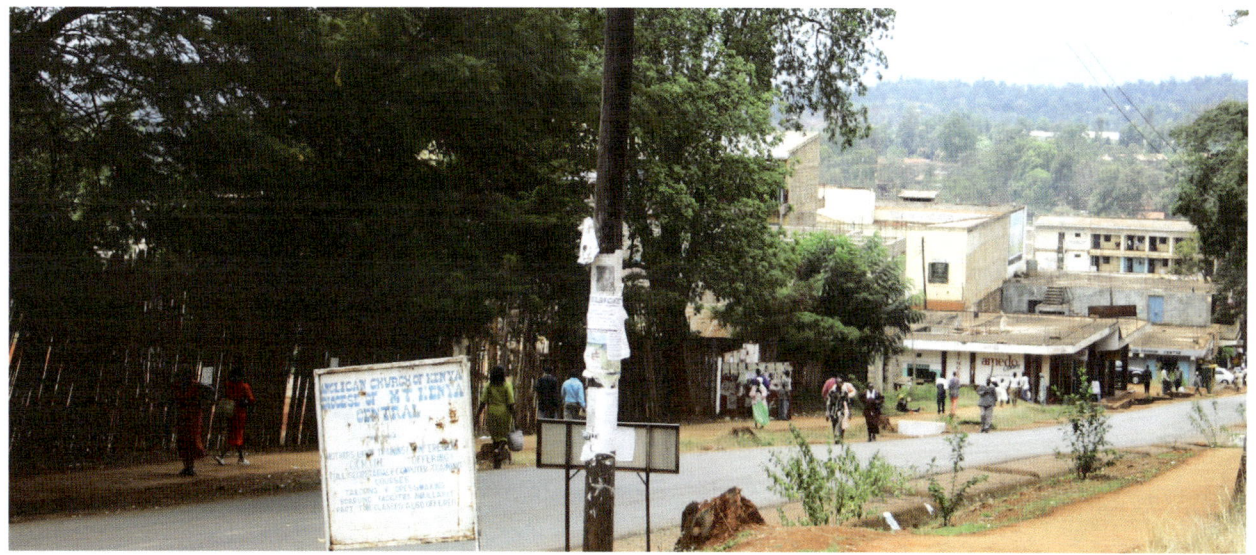
View of Murang'a from Saint James and All Martyrs Memorial Cathedral

For one student, I remember, this meant that the anatomy of cockroaches and beetles became design elements in a long, narrow paper panel she worked on. For others, the subject for sculptures in wood were vultures at rest, like the ones in trees above the butcher shops in Wandagaya, the section of Kampala just outside Makerere's back gate. Barkcloth, a traditional natural fabric common in Uganda, was an occasional canvas for painters.

Njau was not a member of the art department but worked instead as an art educator and teacher trainer, designated an assistant lecturer, in the Demonstration School, a secondary school attached to the Faculty of Education at Makerere.

Nevertheless, he championed the same investigation of material and cultural environments that fueled such art practices among Makerere students. His article 'Copying Puts God to Sleep', published in 1963, encapsulated his thinking about art education in East African schools. If art teachers, he maintained, wanted their students to work inventively and with power, students had to use indigenous materials, materials they were familiar with. In part, that meant that art programmes in schools should not be entirely dependent on the availability of imported supplies. Local clay to mold or to use for marking the way that charcoal and ashes can be used should be brought into classrooms. The frayed ends of sticks might become stippling brushes that students use to create pictures with powdered paint.

The results of this perspective were on display in *Let the Children Paint*, an exhibition of children's art that Njau mounted, first in February 1962 at the Uganda Museum, and subsequently in April at the Sorsbie Gallery in Nairobi. By Christmas time, it was in Germany, in Munich, and later in Frankfurt, Mannheim, Hannover, and Hamburg. It was an exhibition that, in fact, garnered greater attention than undergraduate work in the art department. Full of powerful images, the exhibition declared Njau a gifted teacher, an evaluation easy to arrive at.

If creativity could be stimulated in children, he sensed that perhaps it could be stimulated in fellow artists and in those who aspired to become artists and art teachers. Years later, Njau would work with Wakamba carvers, those who produced slick carvings for the tourist trade. He devised ways to intervene in their ways of working, teaching them to stop their work at midpoints in their usual processes and to see that what they had produced at those intermediate stages would be removed with further carving. Clearly, at Makerere, his ability as a teacher was continually on display, evident to visitors to his classes, both in what he said to students and in the art that his teaching led students to produce. Even though he was not a full-time faculty member in the art department, only a part-time art methods instructor there, all the undergraduates in his teacher training courses were students in the art department; he therefore had an indirect effect on what students produced in the department's studio classes.

What was stimulation for students, however, perhaps became an irritation for some faculty and administrators. Njau was personable, but he was outspoken too, that aspect of personality invigorated by the steady march of the East

African territories toward independence. He questioned the pronouncements of self-professed expatriate experts on African education and culture. Clearly, he imagined a future more accommodating to divergent ideas than Makerere's expatriates seemed willing to acknowledge. It is not surprising, then, that he was viewed as a troubling presence and not invited back to teach at the end of 1961.

Njau's inclination to assert himself was reinforced by the temper of the times. Ideas about black identity, personhood, and political independence that had been alive in the African diaspora for nearly a century were coming to fruition. What was politically imminent for Ghana in 1956 would be a reality for East African territories by 1963. The intellectual and political forces that fostered this social repositioning had equivalence in African American political agitation for racial desegregation. Only the most intellectually isolated among young East Africans were unaware of the turmoil that black people across the American South were experiencing. In the mid-1950s, Little Rock, Arkansas, was identifiable as a place that had meaning for black people around the world. Before the end of the 1960s, dogs, fire hoses, billy clubs, and bombs would have significance, too. Young Americans at Makerere at the beginning of that decade found themselves in the company of young East Africans much like themselves, found commonalities there, even if connections were only tentatively acknowledged. They all knew they were living in times of political flux. Civil rights in the United States had echoes in *uhuru* in East Africa. If young Americans were the proud children of Kennedy, young East Africans had equivalent paternity in Kenyatta, Nyerere, and Obote. High intellectual energy was a product of the times, and Njau enjoyed a sustained measure of it. Whatever this changing political and social reality would finally mean for nations, it energized Njau, established purpose for his labour, a reason to want to project an authentic self, the proper province of a young intellectual.

A clever boy in a forward-looking family, Njau had grown up in Tanzania in circumstances that gave him an early sense of his own worth and his first insights into how art might be used. His father, self-taught, a literate man by 1945 or so, had two sons who preceded Njau as students at Makerere and was himself an unwitting extra spur to Njau's becoming an artist. He had somewhere seen portraits in books when Njau was about twelve and offered a prize to any of his seven sons who could draw the best likeness of him. Njau says that his older brother, Siairuka, who could draw better

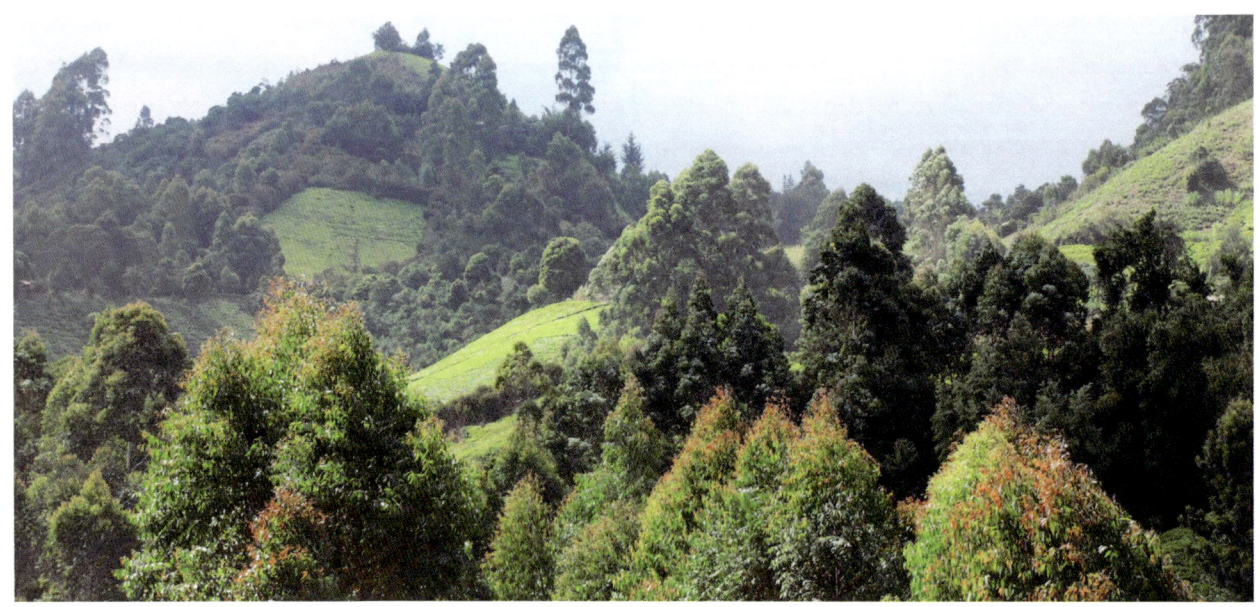

Murang'a County landscape

than he could, would have easily won if he had taken up his father's challenge. He did not, and much to Njau's delight, the portrait he produced, everyone agreed, looked just like his father. That achievement added a dimension to Njau's estimation of himself. His early art experiences generally paralleled those of countless school boys: art activities in a hobby group; no instruction as such, but the supportive presence of a teacher; limited materials, but the occasional use of someone's water colours; in the school library, books about art where paintings were reproduced in colour. But tellingly, throughout his adolescence, he illustrated Bible stories for Sunday school lessons, peopling what he produced with figures that were Africans, that work curiously anticipating the murals he would paint in Murang'a in 1959.

This early illustration work underscored Njau's personal ties to the religiosity of his community and marked a burgeoning awareness that art could be used in its service. His art clearly supported the work of his father, who was a churchman, a lay preacher, and a teacher in a local theological school affiliated with the Lutheran church. The Germans with whom Lutheranism was associated were in Tanzania, then Tanganyika, from the 1880s to World War I, not long enough to have an apparent influence on Njau's generation, so that the church he grew up in was in no way a European church. It never occurred to him to consider it such. During the time that his political and social consciousness developed most significantly – the period after World War II – the church was entirely in the hands of local leaders.

In Njau's youth, in his community, there was, in fact, no church, no building. Services were conducted in a clearing in a forest, among majestic trees, where Heaven had for him a clear point of reference and where sermons focused on the concerns of the community, providing guidance for those who assembled there. What happened on Sundays, Njau says, was an extension of what went on day to day, for the church was a communal space, a place where people worked to create shared reverence and spirituality, necessities for civil living. In that circumstance, Christ, even in the mind of the young Njau, was nearly actual, was a presence almost physical, certainly someone he could have a personal relationship with, someone he could talk to daily and who was, in that, nearly a member of the community.

Having that insight into the nature of his own life, knowing that who he was and how he saw the world were validated and endorsed in a loving family and in a supportive community, was, perhaps, the most significant aspect of Njau's sense of himself. He began to see that he could manage his own internal life, that how he saw himself and the world could be willed and insisted upon. He placed Christ at the centre of what he did daily, so that it was Christ who influenced how he lived and gave him self-confidence. The church, with its association with the institutional and the doctrinaire, did not serve those functions. His sense of himself, anchored in valuing the community that produced him, was what some people responded to when, in his adulthood, they called him charismatic or when others found him a threat to their own sense of who they were.

Njau was among the first diploma graduates of the School of Fine Art at Makerere. Margaret Trowell, a Slade School graduate and the wife of a doctor and researcher, started the school in 1937, and by 1953, over a period of sixteen years, had shepherded the school through a series of administrative structures that moved student credentialing to include a four-year diploma in fine arts with external examinations from the Slade School, in addition to a one-year diploma for teachers of art in schools. Her work as an arts administrator reveals much that made her the remarkable educator that she was. She understood early on the importance of ensuring that students in the fine arts be afforded status through academic course work and examinations that did not distinguish them in negative ways from other Makerere graduates. Perhaps most importantly, Trowell knew that she herself as an outsider had to develop local knowledge to be effective, had to grapple with a complex mix of concerns that art educators in the United Kingdom did not have to confront. Unlike them, for instance, she needed to know how race and culture, hers and students', functioned in the classroom, so that she could create a meaningful context for the Western-style art education she was developing. She sensed that, however her competence increased, East African artists and educators would likely have perspectives that enabled them to provide what she could not. Her long view was that success of the school would rest finally on the contributions that developed from the cross-cultural collaborations that Makerere was fostering.

A measure of what could be realized was revealed in Njau's work as an undergraduate. In 1954, Trowell included some of his work in *And Was Made Man*, a collection of religious paintings, some depicting the life of Christ, images of the kind that would resurface two years later in the preliminary oil sketches he produced for the Murang'a murals. Njau recalls that Trowell was moved by what he had produced. What is particularly notable is that Trowell claims no influence on the African character of his images or of any other student's. As Njau had done in his youth when he drew Sunday school cards in his father's church, when Makerere students produced religious images, the images were black, were "vernacular", to use Trowell's term. Acknowledging how directly religion functioned in African life, she comments that typical religious paintings from the Renaissance that students would have seen had to appear "far off and unreal", so European, so foreign those images would have been for them.

That did not mean that Renaissance images had no value for student artists. Njau certainly saw such images when the youthful John Willings from Manchester joined the Makerere faculty. Willings had a temperament that Njau responded to, and Willings extended the expressiveness that Trowell had always encouraged: power in simplicity, an economy of line used for maximum effect. Much to Njau's liking, also, Willings had an interest in experimentation and in materials that Trowell did not have. Njau recalls Willings directing him to Benvenuto Cellini's book about Renaissance artists and their materials. Willings's instruction in advanced foundational work and his encouraging of experimentation led Njau to learn to grind his own pigments and to use powdered paints like oils. Under Willings's influence, he produced what has been reputed to be the only egg tempera painted by an East African. What he learned about the preparation of surfaces from Willings was invaluable in executing the Murang'a murals.

The murals at Murang'a in Saint James and All Martyrs Memorial Cathedral, then, find their significance in the context of Njau's personal certainty and his acknowledgement of the then-recent political reality, and in the level of his artistry. Scenes from the life of Christ are narrated pictorially in physical and socio-political environments that are identifiably Kenyan. The scenes, five in number, together create a vista, a continuous landscape. Each panel segments the landscape and the right-oriented path through it without destroying continuity. Njau's use of colour assists here. Typically, colours on the right of a panel become colours on the left of a following panel. And since he treats the life of Christ as events unfolding in a single day, through the five panels, he paints a gradually darkening landscape.

The first panel, *Nativity*, presents the birth of Christ in a landscape of abundance under a bright morning sky: a hilly, forested terrain, richly green; thatched *vibanda*, simple round houses, grouped in the far right background; in the lower portion of the panel, a river flows to the right, a road bends to the left. The first political comment is registered here. The clustered houses are Njau's representation of *ujamaa*, the practice of 'villagization', the enactment of the British colonial policy of containment of the Kikuyu in Kenya's Central Province in villages and detention camps during Mau Mau, 1952 to 1959. In one such house, a portion of the wall cut away, stylized to reveal its interior, we see the Nativity, peopled by Kikuyus. Below this scene, wise men ascend the hill, coming to see the newborn. The birth is otherwise unnoted by anyone else. Life in the village simply goes on. Rounding the corner, below the elevated ground, Kikuyu women go to market, following the left-bending road.

An identifiable locale figures prominently in *Baptism of Christ*, the second panel, the depiction of the baptism of Christ by John the Baptist. Njau's Jordan is the Chania Falls, 45 kilometres south of Murang'a, the current site of the Blue Post Hotel in Thika. Recall that, in variation, the four Gospels recount how Jesus came to Galilee to be baptized by John the Baptist and how John was reluctant to do so, believing that Jesus was the prophet that God had sent to baptize the people with the Holy Spirit. Despite his reluctance, he baptized Jesus since he knew that prophecy – "all righteousness" (Matthew 3:15) – had to be fulfilled. Jesus having been baptized, the heavens open, the Spirit of God descends, lighting on Jesus "like a dove" (Matthew 3:16). A voice declares Jesus God's "beloved Son, in whom [He] is pleased" (Matthew 3:17).

Njau does not paint to depict the details that this narrative sequence reveals. On the contrary, he underscores its opposite, the ordinariness of the occurrence. No one in the scene registers awareness of the dimension of what has happened. Capturing the rush of the waterfalls, what Njau in conversation calls their thunder, their natural manifestation, is Njau's way of representing God's revealed power and His rejoicing at Jesus's fulfilling of prophecy. The skill with which he renders the scene honours the wonder that the Gospels record.

The shallow picture plane pushes images to the foreground so that the figure of Christ is the central focus. The concave curve of the riverbank on the right is the parenthetical shape of John the Baptist's wide gesture on the left: his left arm is raised and arched forward; his right arm reaches downward. The lines that these shapes suggest, along with the contour of the pool where Christ stands, nearly encircle Him. The extended verticality of the landscape, the dark rocks over which the water falls, and the downward thrust of trees to the left and right of the falling water further direct this focus on Christ. The pale figures to the right are gathered there simply to witness the baptisms or to be baptized themselves. For them, the dove above Christ's head registers as little as the baptism itself. This is an ordinary scene, and, in this ordinariness, Njau intends a political note, whether it registers or not: the community is unaware of the trouble that lies ahead, as unaware of the power of Mau Mau oath taking as it is of the significance of the baptizing that is represented here.

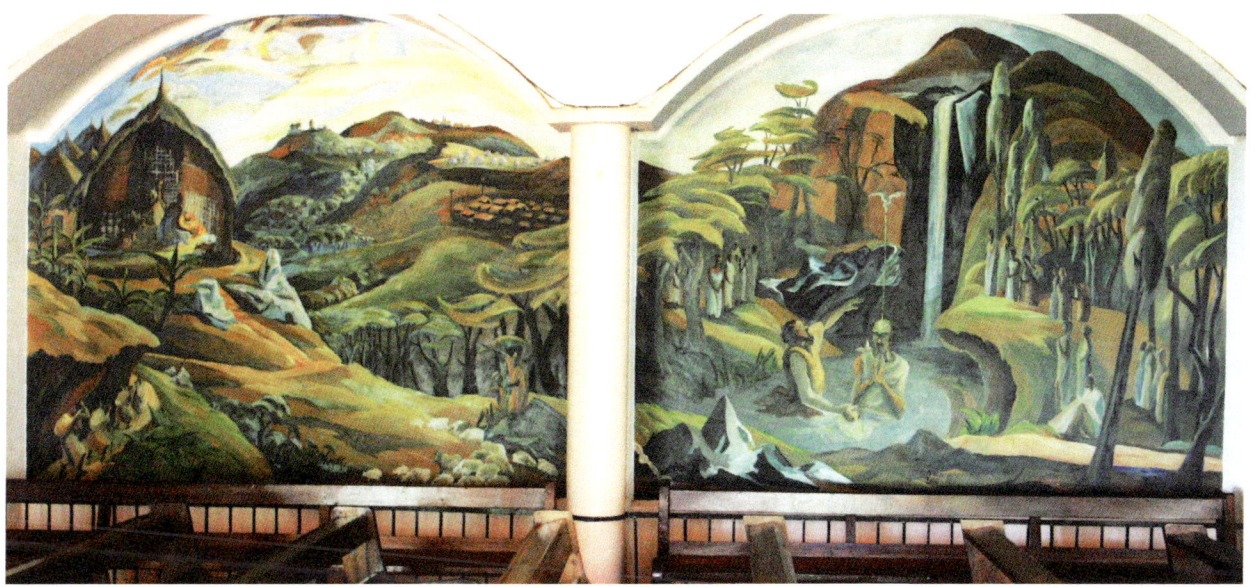

The first two mural panels in the Saint James and All Martyrs Memorial Cathedral

A path at the lower right-hand corner leads to Njau's rendering of *The Last Supper*, the next mural. Here among tall trees, where a giraffe nibbles foliage, Jesus and His disciples gather at a table in an open bungalow, the building stylized in the fashion that one of the *vibanda* in the first panel is, to reveal its interior. A pillar in the middle of the house, with braces placed near its top, resembles a cross, and in this anticipates Calvary and offers a direct visual reference to local Christianity. The disciples are ordinary people, identifiably Kikuyu. Walking sticks, typically carried by Kikuyu men in the countryside, lean against the post. One of them is a *rungu*, a knobbed stick that can be used as a weapon, the likely property of Judas. It stands in contrast to the other sticks and to the long shepherd's stick that is clearly Christ's. They all partake of a local meal: they eat yam instead of bread, drink *njohi* instead of wine, and pass the *njohi* among themselves in a gourd, an *mbotho*, instead of a chalice.

Njau includes a curious oracular element in the scene. In the right-hand corner of the panel, in the lower portion of the mural where the landscape has begun to turn bleak, an owl, a prophetic symbol appropriated from Bantu folklore, signals a troubled present, a sign of the dangers of the times. It is an inclusion rich in its suggestiveness. It resonates for some in the cathedral as a continuing reminder of the temptations of the world, the threats to flesh and spirit that undermine faith and ease the way to perdition. For others among the Christian faithful, certainly in the generation immediately before independence in 1963, trouble and danger specifically recalled the assaultive character of the politics of Mau Mau. While in the popular imagination Mau Mau spelled danger for European settlers, it was, in fact, the African Christian faithful, principally the Kikuyu, who, life and limb, were under sustained threat. They resisted a militant anti-colonialism that accepted violence as necessary to throwing off oppression. They were rejected as individuals overly identified with things European. In consequence, they lived outside the embrace of the community, refusing to participate in cultural practices and invented rituals intended to deepen the community's resolve to claim its humanity and assert its right to self-determination. In their steadfast hold to faith, they were under perpetual, moment-to-moment threat of death. Four thousand such Christians died at the hands of the Mau Mau, a figure that increases in significance when placed beside the 40 European settlers who were killed. This reality is part of what the owl signals and what the murals memorialize.

Associations with Mau Mau become explicit in *Agony in the Garden*, the fourth panel. Jesus, here, is at Gethsemane alone, the disciples, out of sight, resting. The Gospel according to Mark informs us that Jesus agonized. "[T]roubled and deeply distressed", Mark 14: 33 records, Jesus asks God to allow the appointed hour to pass, but even in the asking, Jesus knows that He must die, as prophecy requires. Njau again references the Gospel's narrative only indirectly, but we are aware of a shift in how he depicts Jesus's life, a life now threatened. Njau's figures are oriented in diagonals towards the upper half of the panel. They focus on Jesus. They seem stirred, alert to what is occurring. Danger is made actual. Villages burn. Mount Kenya is angry, the landscape rugged. The physical world becomes the pictorial context that allows Njau a shift in depicting Jesus. Alone among rocks and tall trees, the kneeling Christ is now an angular figure, pale here, nearly transparent, hardly flesh. He seems vulnerable, exposed to danger. Mau Mau, spears in hand, emerge from a cave below an anthill, the anthill aligned with the owl in the preceding panel, offering in this alignment a visual link to the ongoing narrative of violence against Christians.

In *Crucifixion*, the fifth panel, the crucified Christ, high on the picture plane, is a Christ more isolated than previously presented. He is again pale, a transparent presence, the flesh having given way to the spirit. The colours that have built towards the sombre through the five panels underscore an ironic finality here. The sky is a deep dark blue, a night sky, starless without moonlight, but the scene is suffused with light, an intense grey-yellow-orange, not from the sky, but from some subterranean place. In this light, an old man, followed by a small dog, ascends broken steps up to the cross. Mournful women, their bodies bent, are clustered there. Soldiers are among them, as are those who mourn the thieves who have been killed with Christ. These dead are treated in an African way, not crucified but laid out in the open, their dark, desiccated bodies resembling the bare, ravaged trees in the landscape. All the figures in the scene have this same dark cast. Christ, however, is literally beyond the sadness and pain that is represented here. He is grandly triumphal, positioned above those crowded at the foot of the cross. What Njau has chosen to tell of Christ's life is sufficiently complete by this final panel and certainly, in its culmination, a fitting tribute to those in the Christian community martyred for their faith.

These murals are personal readings of the Scriptures, and in their effect, a valediction that connects the plight of Mau Mau–era Christians in Kenya to the trials that biblical Christians endured. In this, Njau is never documentary. He does not paint Africanized aspects of the history of art in the West, although that history was a part of his education at Makerere. The murals are not merely interpretations of Renaissance-derived or Byzantine-inspired scenes from the Bible, either in figuration and composition or in other formal features. It is useful to remind ourselves that religion reflects culture, that religion and culture are always aspects and extensions of each other. The evidence is clearly before us if we simply accept that the religious iconography of the Renaissance, for instance, represents the Europeanization of cultural property generated outside the West. However enduring the normative power of Renaissance iconography

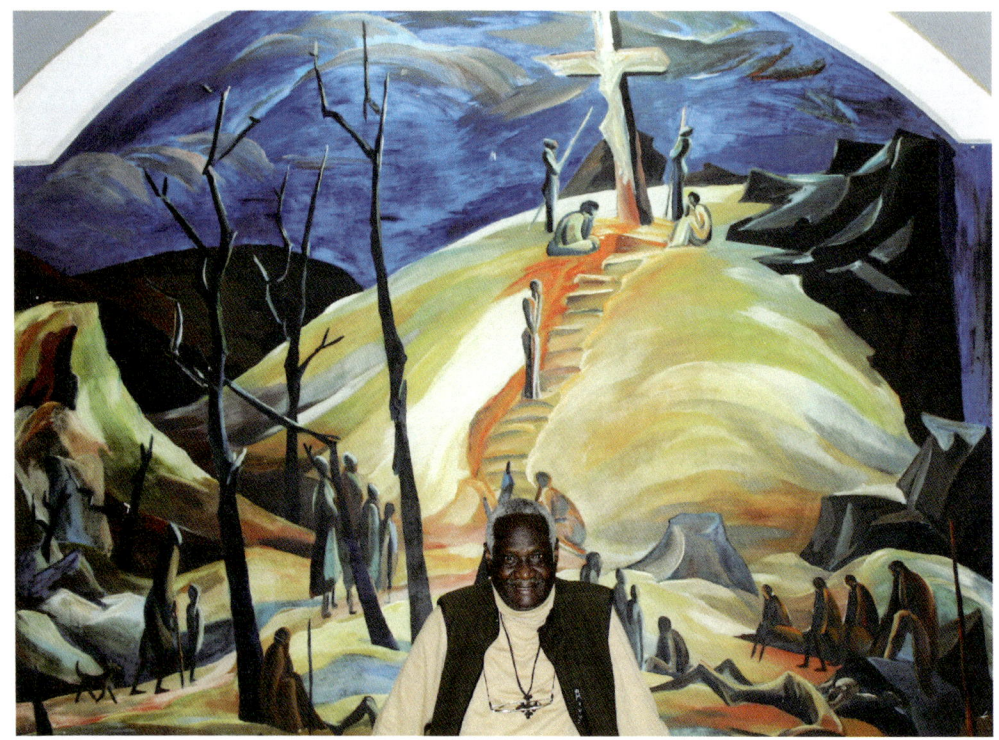

Elimo Njau with the fifth mural panel

remains, it is not a sacrilege to acknowledge that the biblical Holy Land was not an extension of Europe, that fair-skinned people with straight hair were not the representative population. That acknowledgement does not prepare the way for the rejection of Renaissance religious iconography. Instead, it simply reminds us just how effective culture is in reinforcing itself.

What Njau paints, then, is his reality. He does not falsify the gesture, reaching for political grandeur. The murals are not religious-oriented proletarian tributes to heroes in Kenya's struggle for self-rule, reflecting traditions of representation rooted in European social realism. There are no heroes. Jomo Kenyatta and Dedan Kimathi, Kenyans routinely identified with the Mau Mau political insurgency, are no more present than is Jesus with a gaze invented by Roselli or imagined by an unnamed painter of icons in Constantinople in 400 AD. Anonymity embraces everyone, everything. Martyred Kenyans could have been painted as recognizable members of the community but were not. Church officials at the cathedral, in a similar vein, determined that a mural, especially one like the fifth panel depicting the Crucifixion, should not be placed behind the pulpit. Placed there, the Crucifixion, to their minds, would have an inappropriate prominence, would hold the attention of congregants in ways akin to idolatry. Njau endorsed their decision and extended anonymity even to the completed work itself. The murals [originally] had no attribution. Njau did not sign them. They were God's work. Signing them, he said, would have been like signing one's offspring. ‡

PAA YA PAA AND THE ART SCENE IN EAST AFRICA

Terry Hirst

IN 1956, during the 'State of Emergency' in Kenya, the Anglican Church of East Africa was commissioning murals for Christian churches throughout the province from the first formally trained artists from Makerere University. Rekyaelimoo (Elimo) Njau's mural series of five panels, in the Saint James and All Martyrs Memorial Cathedral at Fort Hall (now Murang'a), was part of a significant socio-cultural transformation. For it represented a complete break with the religious images in Africa that had prevailed until Njau's generation.

It also represented a drastic break, generally, with the church's pantheon of images characterizing mural painting in Europe. Elimo himself was a second generation Christian, with his father, Phillipo Njau, having been one of the first

Dedicated to
All those concerned about culture and life in Africa.
Let us strive to be real men and women and not unique artists!
Let us revive the cultural life of our people.
Let our art, music, drama, literature and architecture be the cement
of our Community but with a new spiritual light glowing through them.
Let us all strive to build a real and living visual image of God here
in Africa.

Introduction in *The Fort Hall Murals: The Life of Christ in Pictures*, published in 1963, reflecting the philosophy of Kibo Art Gallery and Paa ya Paa Art Centre

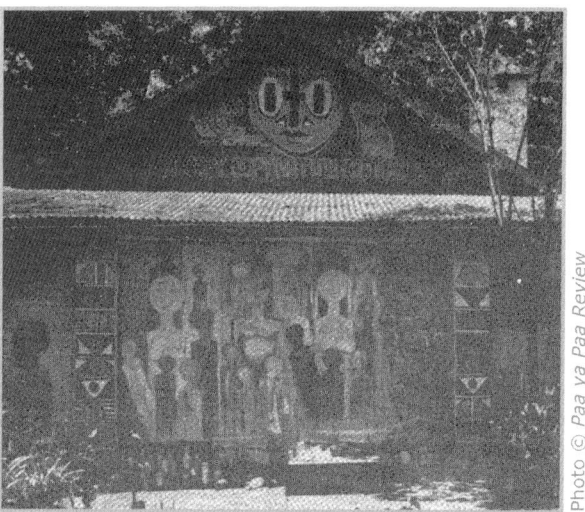
Paa ya Paa Art Centre in Ridgeways Estate in the 1960s

African Lutheran lay preachers in the Kilimanjaro region of Tanzania.

As the emergency ended and independence approached in East Africa, there was still much tension and bitterness as local artists fought for recognition. In Kenya, the Chemchemi Cultural Centre was established in Nairobi in 1961. It was among the earliest institutions catering for trained artists and their artistic creations. Centrally placed on Mfungano Street, Nairobi, it became fully operational in 1963.

Chemchemi attracted the newly formed Community of East African Artists, led by Sam Ntiro, Elimo Njau, and Eli Kyeyune, to operate under its umbrella. Elimo Njau, one of the original founders, was named as the first local African director of the centre, but he resigned almost immediately because of misgivings related to funding from the Congress for Cultural Freedom.

After a time of association with Chemchemi, Njau formed the Paa ya Paa Art Gallery, located on Loita Street, Nairobi. The founding group of the emerging Paa ya Paa Art Centre was made up of Elimo and Rebecca Njau, Hilary Ng'weno, James Kangwana, Jonathan Kariara, Charles and Primila Lewis, and Dr. Rogoff, formerly the Chief Police Pathologist during the Emergency, soon to be joined by Terry Hirst.

By the mid-1960s, the Paa ya Paa Art Gallery was provocatively introducing the values of 'modern art' to Kenya. The emergence of Paa ya Paa coincided with founding of Rajat Neogy's groundbreaking and seminal intellectual journal *Transition*, and the publication of Okot p'Bitek's *Song of Lawino*, destined to become a classic.

It was a very exciting time. The friends at Paa ya Paa were joined by Nereas Gicoru, Pheroze and Villoo Nowrojee, Ray Catchpole, and Joanna Cammaerts. In 1970, Phillda Ragland, who later became Phillda Ragland Njau, came to administer the Paa ya Paa Art Centre in Ridgeways – a leafy suburb in Nairobi North – after managing the Kibo Art Gallery in Marangu, Tanzania, for some time.

Paa ya Paa provided exhibition space for young artists, both formally and informally trained, with well-publicized gallery openings, well-written, illustrated catalogues, and a good sales service. It was also identified as a "major literary movement of the time", featuring Okot p'Bitek's 'Bush Nights', begun in 1967, during which he narrated African folk tales. These nights grew into regular poetry recitals, with drum and often jazz accompaniment.

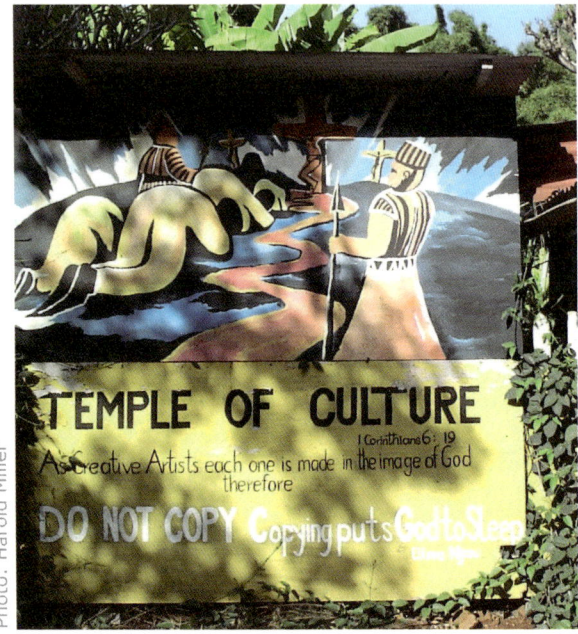

Sign at Paa ya Paa Art Centre, 2008

Ngugi wa Thiong'o was an active Paa ya Paa participant even as he was organizing and writing for his own creative theatre venture in Kamarithu Village near Limuru. The journal of creative writing *Zuka*, edited by Jonathan Kariara, was launched at Paa ya Paa in 1967 and carried work by all the leading writers of the day, including Okot p'Bitek, Ama ata Aidoo, Taban lo Liyong, John Ruganda, Marjorie Oludhe Macgoye, and Ngugi, who later became co-editor with Kariara. Hilary Ng'weno wrote later, "The major literary movement of the time was in many ways associated with what might be called the 'Paa ya Paa School'. Apart from the literary and intellectual movement centred around the Kampala-based bimonthly *Transition*, Paa ya Paa was the main focus of creativity in East Africa in the '60s."

As an art gallery, Paa ya Paa became well known internationally, with exhibitions going abroad to places such as the National Gallery in Zambia, the prestigious Commonwealth Institute in London, and commercial galleries in Soho, New York. It received exhibitions from West Africa, Ethiopia, Sudan, and West Germany, as well as support from a wide variety of international writers, artists, and performers, who all gave fascinating talks and spontaneous performances at the gallery. They included personalities such as Walter Rodney, Sidney Poitier, Dick Gregory, Cameron Duodo, Clayton Pond, Edward Braithewaite, Alvin Ailey and his American Dance Theatre, and Wole Soyinka. Soyinka's new play *The Strong Breed* had premiered in 1966 at the Kenya National Theatre, directed by Jonathan Kariara, who worked with the Paa ya Paa Theatre Group.

But without direct donor funding, the burden on the original founders became too acute. During the early 1970s, the Paa ya Paa Gallery survived fitfully, operating a kind of café-cum-art gallery managed by Josephine Kamau. Then an extraordinary thing happened, changing the very nature of Paa ya Paa. A fine old colonial farmhouse located in Ridgeways Estate, just north of Nairobi, was put on sale. A former teacher of Njau's arranged the finance for the purchase of the five-acre property. So, in 1975 Paa ya Paa acquired a new and expansive 'home', located on what Nairobi City Council later named Paa ya Paa Lane. A whole new era of cultural activity opened.

A 1990 issue of *Paa ya Paa Review*, edited by Debra Martens, on the occasion of the twenty-fifth anniversary of the gallery, contains Elimo Njau's 'faith statement' with regard to art:

"When I finished my studies at Makerere University, I was puzzled by the contemporary artistic chaos in East Africa. I said to myself, 'Here I am with all my qualifications, both as an artist and teacher, but I don't really know where I am. How can I teach my students art, if I don't know where I am going?' My quest, I decided, was to find a philosophy to guide me. I looked for this philosophy in modern Western art, in vain; I searched for it in traditional African art, and found a powerful symbolism and a portion of the sense of purpose I sought; I looked for it in contemporary Asian artists and critics of East Africa, and found them just as confused and lost as myself. At last, one day, I saw that the pumpkins in my mother's garden were never exactly alike. I looked at my sister, and she was not exactly like my mother.

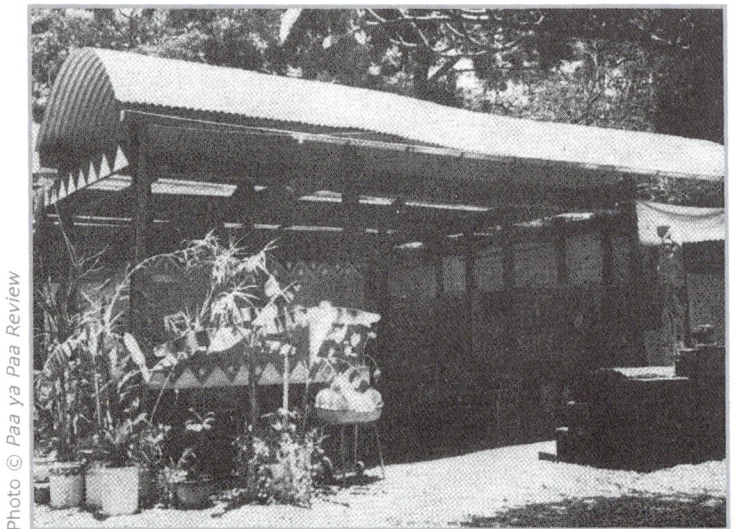

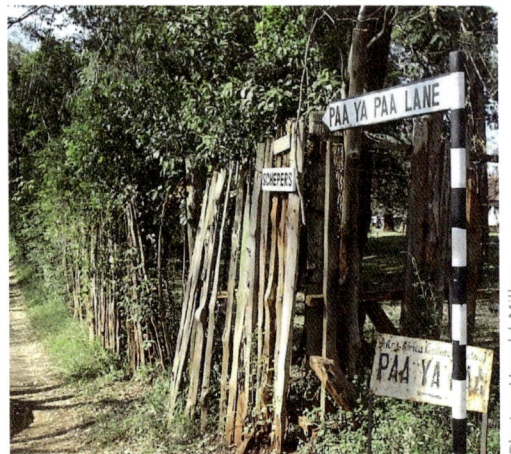

Exhibition area of Paa ya Paa Art Centre in Ridgeways in the 1970s and Paa ya Paa Lane

I examined myself in a mirror and found that I was not identical to my father or grandfather. If every new baby was a new creation, then why should I copy anybody? I had discovered God's creative secret. Since God is omnipotent as well as omnipresent, then He must be in me and His power must be in me, because he did not create me in the image of anybody else but Himself. In all my creative efforts, therefore, I must keep Him alive. I believed that as time went on, He would be so much part of me that I would be able to fill up Africa with vigorous and fertile young artists who would prove to the world God's full presence in Africa. For my own guidance and as a warning to my students and fellow artists I formulated the following policy: DO NOT COPY; COPYING PUTS GOD TO SLEEP. It has guided us to this day at Paa ya Paa."

In December 1997, the Paa ya Paa venture came to an abrupt end, when the whole of the Ridgeway farmhouse and the gallery burned down one tragic night. The whole of the Paa ya Paa permanent collection of paintings, prints, drawings, wood carvings, and ceramics – quite literally the whole 32-year history of modern art in East Africa – had gone up in smoke, along with all the records, books, films, tapes, and videos that had vouched for their existence.

A long article in the *East African Standard* quoted Njau, then still in hospital recovering from smoke inhalation:

"Elimo Njau described the calamity as a purification ceremony. 'This was a purification ceremony. In August I suffered severe burns in my groins when I turned on my faulty shower tap. A jet of boiling water washed my groins and peeled off my skin. And now El Niño has taken its toll on me. I think El Niño, that means the Child Christ, has decided to purify me. There is more happiness in being alive than in material things,' he said with tears falling from his ever-welling eyes. Njau is currently partially blind and sees huge blurs for a person. Njau collapsed as he tried to recover three sketches of Jesus Christ that he had been commissioned to paint by the Murang'a Anglican Cathedral. They were entitled the 'Resurrection', 'Ascension' and 'Judgment'. Elimo now says he will conduct storytelling sessions for children to earn a living and will construct a tin house to shelter his family. 'I have no choice. I now have to start a new future without a past. I will construct a tin house to live in temporarily. Too much of what we have is not good for us. You see God is my only insurance,' he said as he tried to gather courage to smile. The old Mau Mau statue at the main entrance still towers over the rubble of the gallery. And the lush green forest of trees gives one the impression that all is calm."

But now, everything had changed utterly. However, Paa ya Paa is not "a future without a past", because it may now be a museum of cultural heritage, rather than just an art gallery, epitomizing all that is inherent in the juxtaposition of the two outstanding creative works enshrined there: Elimo Njau's dramatic mural sketches from the Saint James and All Martyrs Memorial Cathedral in Murang'a, and Sam Wanjau's triumphant *Freedom Fighter*. Both of these works are still largely unrecognized by the current dominant narrative about art in Kenya. In them are embedded important issues of social, political, and religious identity, still to be resolved and reconciled.

‡

ABOUT REKYAELIMOO (ELIMO) PHILIPO NJAU

Phillda Ragland Njau

YES! The man behind the murals, Elimo Njau, finally embraced the name his parents bestowed on him 82 years ago – Rekyaelimoo, which means 'dedicate your soul to God'. Fifty years after painting the life of Christ as portrayed through an African landscape, he signed the murals with his real name, which the colonialists had shortened so they would be able to pronounce it more easily.

The murals were popularized in religious communities in the West in the early 1960s when I first learned of him while working in overseas communications for the headquarters of the United Presbyterian Church, USA, in New York City. The church had already produced a film called *Harambee*, which featured the emerging talents of artists from developing nations, specifically Asia and Africa. Njau and his work and words were highlighted, and in religious circles he was hailed as East Africa's foremost Christian artist, owing to the amount of works he had already created on religious themes. In the 1950s, the churches of Africa had already led the way in commissioning sculptors and artists to use their skill and understanding in nation building. *Christ in the Art of Africa* and *The Holy Family in the Art of Africa and Asia* were two filmstrips that included paintings and sculptures of Njau's creation, and both were suggested as good resources to promote the Christian mission among new nations of the day.

In the film *Harambee*, Njau is seen speaking from his studio in Nairobi: "An artist without a faith is like a hoe without a handle. What can he do? He can only scratch the surface of the soil. True art draws from the soil and the community

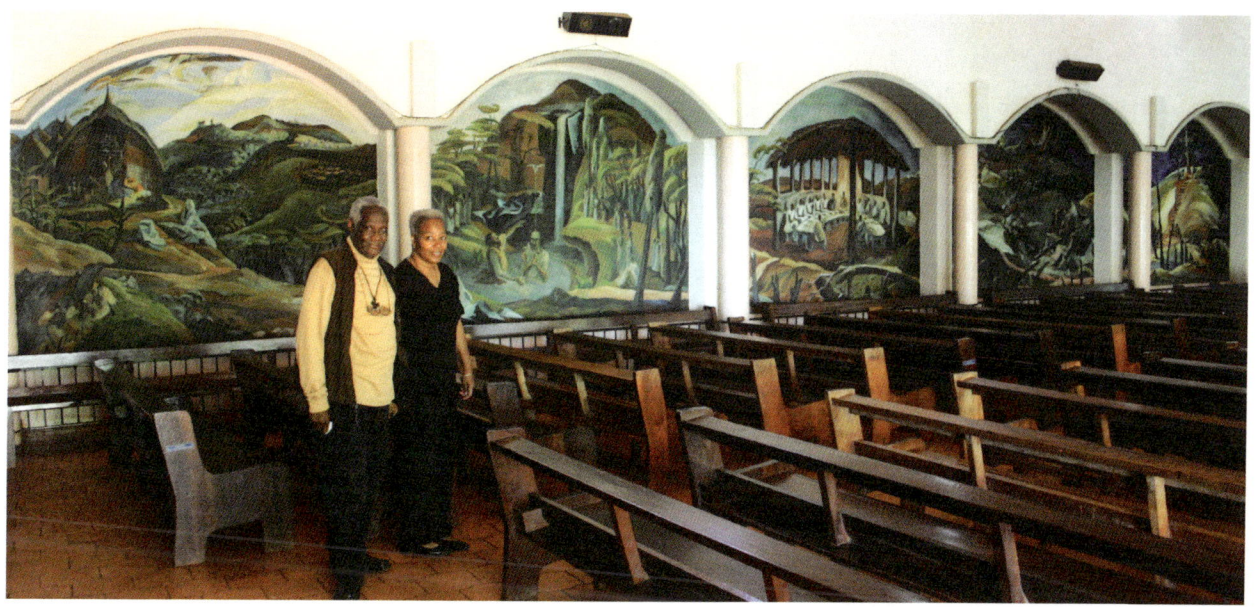

Elimo Njau and Phillda Njau in the Saint James and All Martyrs Memorial Cathedral

in which we live. None of us can pretend to be more ahead of our time than Christ. We must never escape the call to live more fully and truly in our surroundings, always with our eyes focused on God's call to all the true children of Africa." This statement aptly summarizes the artist's thoughts about his own personal faith and art. What follows is a summary of Njau's life journey and achievements.

Rekyaelimoo Philipo Njau was born on 24 August 1932 in Marangu village near Mount Kilimanjaro in Tanzania. He attended the Makerere School of Fine Art in Kampala in 1953, receiving a Diploma of Fine Art in 1957 and a Diploma of Education in 1958. Njau went on to become one of the region's best-known artists, over the years serving as a teacher and a lecturer, as well as a motivational speaker on African cultural values. He was founder and director of Kibo Art Centre in Marangu, Tanzania. In Nairobi, he founded Chemchemi Cultural Centre with South African writer Es'kia Mphahlele. Soon after, he was a founding member of Paa ya Paa Art Centre; he has been director of the centre for many years. In 1962, Njau was also assistant director of Sorsbie Gallery in Nairobi. He has taught or lectured at Makerere University, University of Dar es Salaam, Kenyatta University, and United States International University.

Aside from Paa ya Paa exhibitions, Njau has had the following solo exhibitions:
- Uganda Museum, *Landscapes of Kampala and Entebbe*, Kampala (1960)
- Commonwealth Institute, London (1961)
- Sorsbie Gallery, Nairobi, Kenya (1962)
- Indian High Commission, Nairobi (1966)
- Chemchemi Cultural Centre, Nairobi (1992)
- Mashiriki Gallery, Nairobi (1994)

In addition, he has participated in a variety of noteworthy group exhibitions:
- All Africa Conference of Churches Assembly, Kenyatta Conference Centre, Nairobi (1975)
- East African Commonwealth Exhibition, London (1984)
- Freedom From Hunger, *Art Fights Hunger*, Sarit Centre, Nairobi (1985)
- *The Child in Contemporary Art*, French Cultural Centre, Nairobi (1986)
- *Art in Daily Life*, Sarit Centre, Nairobi (1990)
- Thanksgiving and Rededication of Paa Ya Paa Art Centre, Nairobi (2002)

Over the years, Njau has organized numerous exhibitions, art projects, and conferences. These included an exhibition tour of children's art in East Africa and West Germany, a Christian Arts Exhibition in Zambia, workshops and exhibitions at Nairobi's Goethe Institute, Freedom from Hunger exhibitions at Nairobi's Sarit Centre, the East African Commonwealth Exhibition in London, and the Agricultural Society of Kenya's International Trade Show in Nairobi.

Paa ya Paa Art Centre and Kibo Art Centre staged various exhibitions in the region, conducted workshops, and collaborated widely. The two centres put on competitions such as the All Africa Christmas Card Competition and festivals such as the All Africa Cultural Festival, the Annual Mother Christmas Festival, and the Year of the Child celebrations. Njau was involved in two TV programmes: *Utamaduni Kwa Watoto* and *Brains Trust* for Voice of Kenya TV.

The following murals are Njau's major works:
- The Murang'a murals on the life of Christ
- Nativity painting now at Kibo Art Centre
- Mural for the Bank of Tanzania
- Mural of *The Baptism of Christ* at Anglican Church, Tanga, Tanzania
- Mural of *St. Francis of Assisi with the Animals of East Africa* at St. Francis Chapel, Makerere College, Kampala

Apart from regular newsletters, Njau and the two art centres produced a number of publications, including *The Scar*, *The Green Bean Patch*, *Makonde Sculpture*, *Art Master's Hobby*, *Let the Children Paint*, and *African Art*.

Finally, throughout his colourful career Elimo Njau has been the recipient of various scholarships, sponsorships, awards, prizes, and distinctions:
- First prize for book cover design competition (*Miti ni Mali* series) organized by the East African Literature Bureau
- First prize for designing the Chagga flag and the Chagga Crest for the Chagga Council in Moshi, Tanzania
- Fine art prize in painting for second-year work in art school
- One-month tour of Germany and Sweden, sponsored by the Lutheran Church of West Germany
- Judge for Zimbabwe's International Art Competition and contributor to Zimbabwe Heritage Magazine, Harare, Zimbabwe
- Uganda Independence Medal for outstanding service to the country in art education at Makerere University, Kampala
- Selection of Paa ya Paa Art Centre as a host site for the New York-based Arts International Artist-in-Residence Programme

‡

BIBLIOGRAPHY

Anderson, David. *The Histories of the Hanged: The Dirty War in Kenya and the End of Empire*, London, W. W. Norton & Company, 2005.

Anglican Church of Kenya. *Church Workers Directory,* Nairobi, Uzima Press, 2007.

Department of Information, Kenya Colony. 'The Fort Hall Memorial Church', an article in *The Archbishop of Canterbury's Tour of Kenya: The Official Record of the Archbishop's Tour* [May 1955], London, Pitkin Pictorials Ltd., n.d.

Foster, James. 'The Memorial Church at Fort Hall', a specially commissioned essay, Nairobi, April 2007.

Frost, Richard. *Race Against Time: Human Relations and Politics in Kenya Before Independence*, London, Rex Collings, 1978.

Jones, William. 'Personality, Religion, and Politics in the Art of Elimo Njau: The Murals at Murang'a', a public lecture presented on 13 September 2006 at All Africa Conference of Churches, Nairobi.

Kariuki, Obadiah. *A Bishop Facing Mount Kenya: An Autobiography 1902–1978* (translated from the Kikuyu by George Mathu), Nairobi, Uzima Press, 1985.

Koigi, John. 'Njau Finally Signs His Paintings', *Saturday Nation*, 2 December 2006.

Matheson, Alastair (editor). 'Church of the Martyrs', *Kenya Today,* Vol. 4, No. 4, p. 10, published by the Department of Information of the Government of Kenya, Nairobi, December 1958.

Mount, Marshall Ward. *African Art: The Years since 1920*, 'Chapter 4: Art Schools in English-speaking East and Central Africa', p. 95–101, Indiana University Press, 1973.

Nowrojee, Pheroze. 'The Fort Hall Murals of Elimo Njau', Nairobi, 2006.

Oliver, Roland. *The Missionary Factor in East Africa*, London, Longmans, Green & Co., 1952.

Omondi, Deo. 'Paa ya Paa Burned Down', *East African Standard*, 10 December 1997.

Stinton, Diane. 'Jesus-Immanuel, Image of the Invisible God: Aspects of Popular Christology in Sub-Saharan Africa', *Journal of Reformed Theology I* (reproduced with special permission from BRILL, publisher of the *Journal of Reformed Theology*), Leiden, 2007.

The Fort Hall Murals: The Life of Christ in Pictures, Nairobi, Paa ya Paa/Kibo Art Gallery, 1963.

The Times [of London]. 'African Artist's Church Murals: Memorial to Victims of Mau Mau', 11 October 1958.

Trowell, K. Margaret. *And Was Made Man: The Life of Our Lord in Pictures*, London, SPCK, 1956.

Related Resources

Gatu, John G. *Joyfully Christian – Truly African*, Nairobi, Acton Publishers, 2006.

Smoker, Dorothy (compiler/editor). *Ambushed by Love: God's Triumph in Kenya's Terror*, Fort Washington, PA, Christian Literature Crusade-USA, 1993.

POSTSCRIPT

African Artist's Church Murals: Memorial to Victims of Mau Mau

In the new Church of the Martyrs at Fort Hall, Kenya, built as a memorial to the victims of Mau Mau terrorists, Elimo Njau, a young Chagga artist, [is painting] five large murals depicting the life of Christ, against a Kikuyuland background. The church, designed by Mr. Julian Hill, is to be consecrated to-morrow.

The Times (London), 11 October 1958

Njau Finally Signs His Paintings
by John Koigi

After a 50-year wait, veteran artist Elimo Njau has finally appended his signature to the murals at St. James' Anglican Cathedral in Kiharu, Murang'a. In a relatively low-key event presided over by Vicar Jesse Ngure, Njau, the founder of Paa ya Paa Arts Centre, put to rest doubts regarding the person behind the five paintings that tell the story of Jesus Christ.

Saturday Nation, 2 December 2006

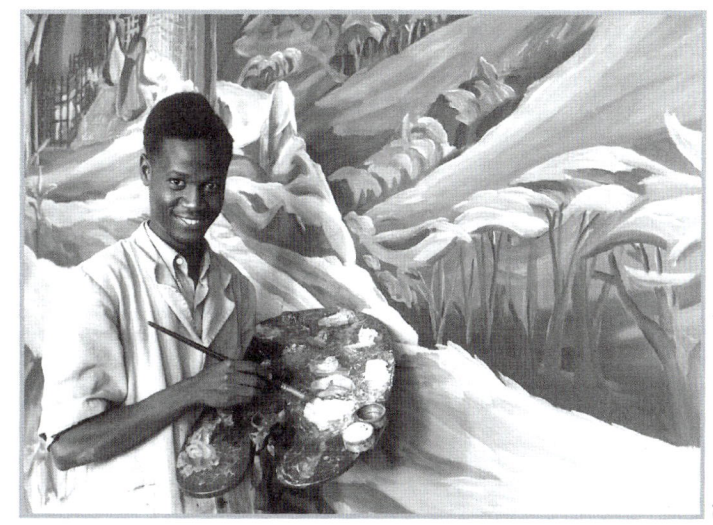

Photo: Department of Information, Kenya Colony

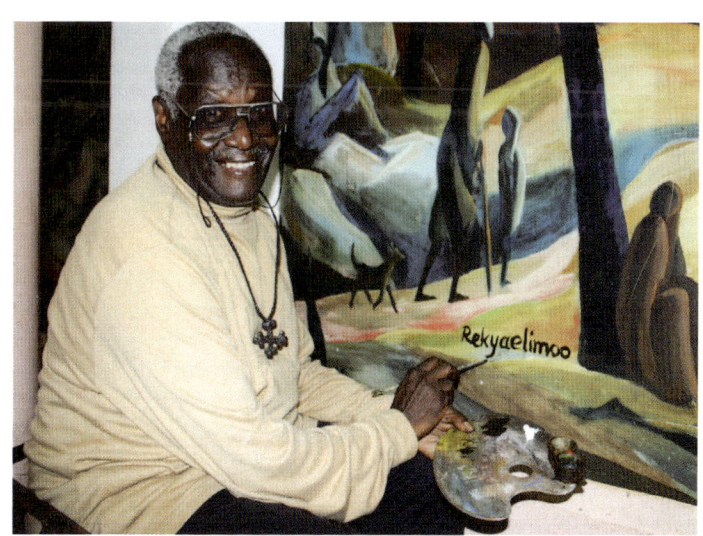

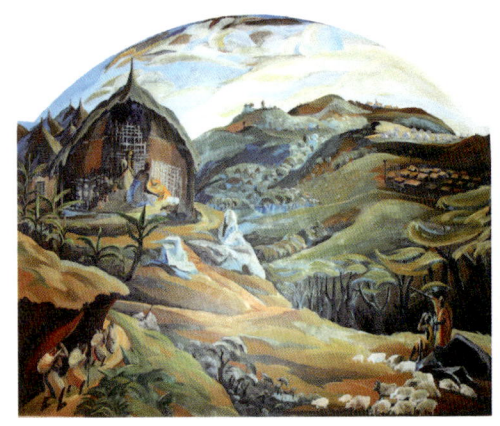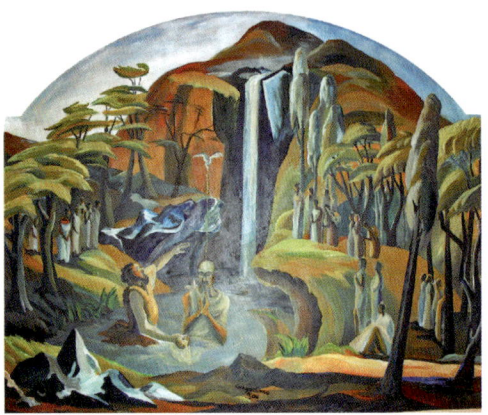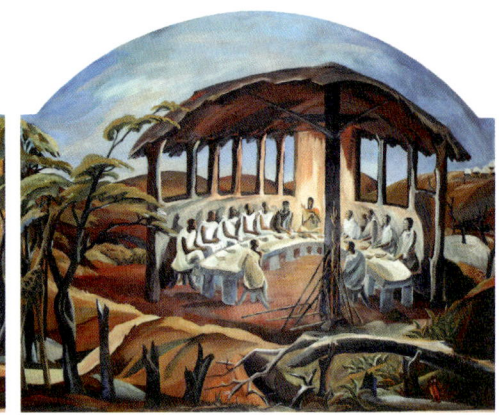

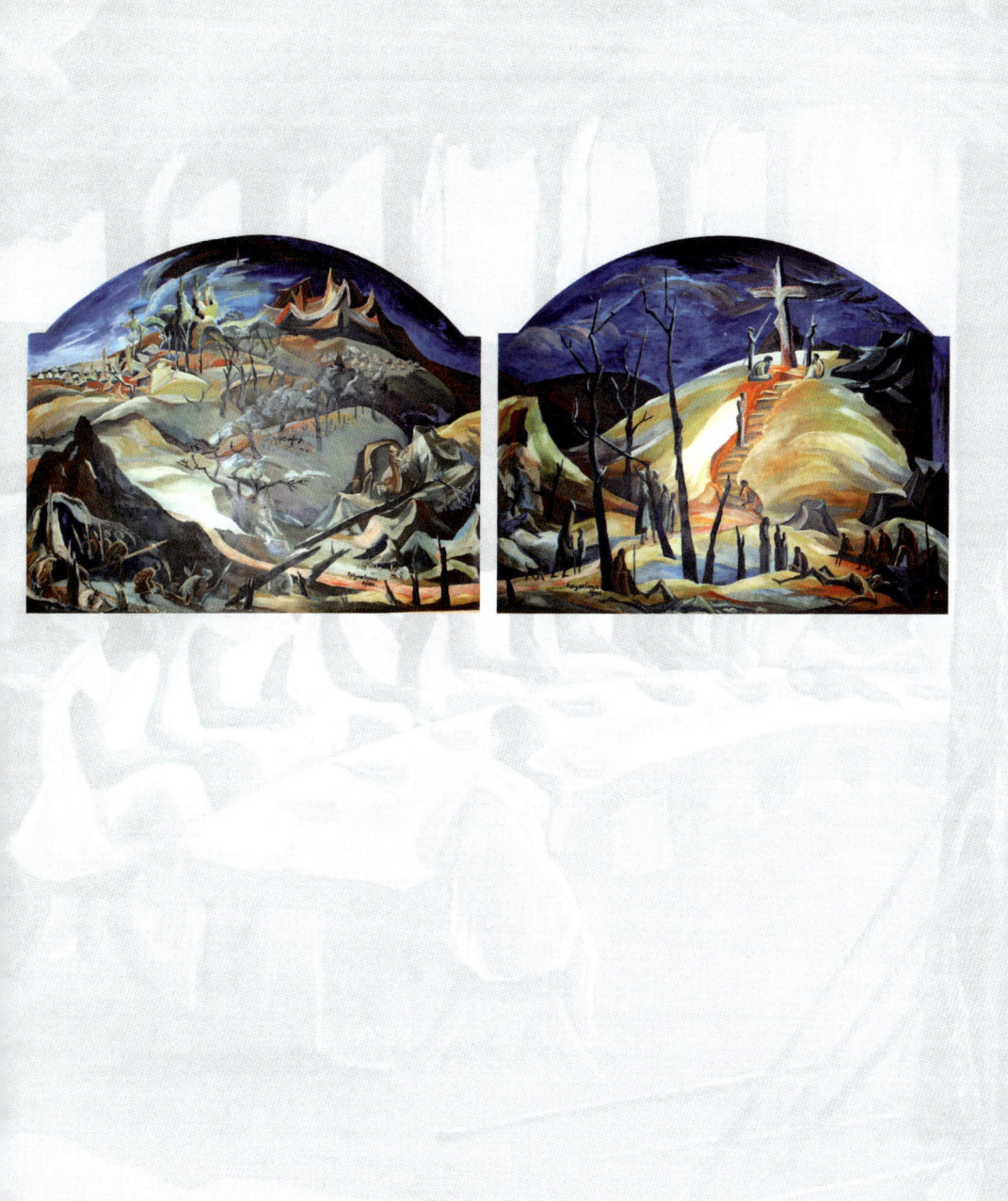

Made in the USA
Charleston, SC
08 February 2015